PICKETT'S CHARGE:

The Untold Story

PICKETT'S CHARGE:

The Untold Story

BRUCE E. MOWDAY

[signature: Bruce E. Mowday]

Published by Barricade Books Inc.
2037 Lemoine Ave.
Suite 362
Fort Lee, NJ 07024
www.barricadebooks.com

Library of Congress Cataloging-in-Publication Data

Mowday, Bruce.
    Pickett's charge : the untold story / by Bruce E. Mowday.
        pages cm
    Includes bibliographical references and index.
    ISBN: 978-1-56980-508-4
    1. Gettysburg, Battle of, Gettysburg, Pa., 1863. 2. Webb, Alexander S.
(Alexander Stewart), 1835-1911. 3. United States. Army. Philadelphia
Brigade (1861-1865) 4. Pickett, George E. (George Edward), 1825-1875.
I. Title.
    E475.53.M925 2013
    973.7'349--dc23
                                                                2013013892
                    ISBN: 978-1-56980-508-4

        10 9 8 7

Manufactured in the United States of America

DEDICATION

Pickett's Charge: The Untold Story is dedicated to everyone involved in preserving this nation's rich Civil War history for future generations. Historians, writers, re-enactors, history teachers and the countless members of the public interested in delving into the details of the War between the States should be applauded and encouraged.

CONTENTS

FOREWORD

W HEN ASKED TO what he attributed the failure of the Confederates at Gettysburg, Major General George E. Pickett, CSA is said to have answered, "I think the Union Army had something to do with it." While undoubtedly correct, the quip is unsatisfying because it offers no reason for Union success or Southern failure. The story of the Union defense of Cemetery Ridge offers reasons.

This book might be properly titled *Webb's Stand at the Angle*, but then much of the public would not recognize the topic because that is not how the encounter is celebrated or remembered. Today called "Pickett's Charge," several historians convincingly argue that the name, at a stroke, not only removes the Union army from the scene but also other Confederate participants. As currently understood, Pickett's Charge is largely the Virginian memory and interpretation of events, expressing a Confederate, that is to say Southern, view of the fight. This view is widely accepted by the public. Commercially successful fictional works such as Michael Shaara's *Killer Angels* (1974) and the film based on that book, *Gettysburg* (1993) bear witness to that cultural acceptance. Further complicating matters for purists, numerous accounts written by veterans on both sides do not agree, making establishment of incontrovertible tactical detail impossible.

Although disagreeing on the details, Civil War authorities might agree on four themes. First, the Confederate charge of July 3 was the pivotal episode of the three day fight. Second, after a long record of failure, victory was won by the Army of the Potomac. Third and conversely, the Army of Northern Virginia bore the unaccustomed burden of defeat. Last, over time and in hindsight, the repulse of the charge became recognized as an event marking the end of doubts about the resolution of the Civil War, signifying the ultimate failure of the Confederacy, the eventual end of the war, and the continuation of the republic.

To bring clarity and order and thus understanding and meaning out of the chaos of combat and memory, writers of military historical narrative often tell their tale from a particular point of view. Bruce Mowday reminds us that, for the Union to prevail over a heroic, gallant, and desperate Confederate assault, required an equally heroic, gallant, and desperate defense.

He uses the words of the Union participants to relate events and describe that defense. By drawing on Union memory, the tale includes Union controversies and ultimately, the Union interpretation of the climatic event of the battle as well as the meaning behind personal sacrifice.

Perhaps less well understood is that readers of history, also attempting to make sense of chaotic events, select historical material that becomes their individual interpretation of events from which they draw meaning. My personal connection to the battle of Gettysburg begins in the late 1960s when, as a teenager and after reading about the three day battle, I undertook a solo road trip in late winter to see the battlefield for myself and make up my own mind about events. At the almost abandoned National park, over a home-made box lunch, I surveyed Cemetery Ridge, the Copse of Trees, the Angle, and the wide fields extending west to the wooded Seminary Ridge. The visit, although leaving an indelible impression, provided no clear answers, only the idea, almost just a feeling, of what must have happened at this place on a hot July afternoon. As they charged under fire across the field, something held the Confederate soldiers in closed ranks, and something also held the Union soldiers in their ranks, largely in position behind a much too low stone wall, to await assault by thousands of aroused Confederates. Even to the casual observer it is obvious what must have happened in the small space of ground defended by Brigadier General Alexander S. Webb's Philadelphia Brigade during the final minutes of the charge. Rather than a destination, the trip was one of the first steps of a longer continuing personal journey. Since then, on numerous occasions, I have revisited both the battlefield and my interpretation of events. In every case, the experience is awe inspiring. Assessing myths and facts surrounding the battle in *Pickett's Charge in History and Memory* (1997), Carol Reardon, Ph.D., Professor of American History, Penn State University points out that just what is awe inspiring "remains essentially an individual matter."

Bruce Mowday's *Pickett's Charge: The Untold Story* (2013) brings to light a large number of largely ignored or forgotten narratives provided by Union participants of all ranks, often taken from a personal letter or testimony. Much of the material is frequently overlooked by other writers because, being kept in archives and unavailable in digital form, the artifacts can be difficult for authors to consult. In this book, Bruce takes his readers along with him in an inspiring journey to hear from the veterans themselves the reasons for Union victory.

Dave Burford, M.A.
Military History,
Norwich University, 2012
Independent Scholar
October 2012

ACKNOWLEDGEMENTS

A NY WRITER UNDERTAKING a project involving Gettysburg must have access to a small army of historical experts. The pivotal battle of the American Civil War has been studied, dissected and chronicled for 150 years. No one person in one lifetime could ever duplicate all of the research that has been compiled since July 3, 1863.

I have many people to thank for helping with this project and I should start with the staff at Gettysburg National Military Park, especially John Heiser, park historian. John spent many hours guiding me through the park records housed in the research library. He answered my questions and he introduced me to other knowledgeable members of the national park staff. He also checked the manuscript for historical errors and made many excellent suggestions dealing with the historical perspective of the outcome of the battle of Gettysburg.

West Chester, Pennsylvania, business colleague Laura Burford introduced me to her husband David, a military scholar and former military officer. I spent a very interesting lunch with David going over tactics and also delving into the motivations of the soldiers engaged at Pickett's Charge. David also authored the foreword to this book and reviewed the manuscript with a critical eye. His insights were very valuable. David also introduced me a book on the myths of Gettysburg.

During my numerous trips to Gettysburg National Military Park to conduct research, I spoke with park rangers and volunteers. They all were always gracious and accommodating to my requests. Ranger Scott Hartwig, supervisory historian at Gettysburg, talked with me early in my research about the battle and gave me some excellent and appreciated guidance. I joined the Friends of Gettysburg, affiliated with the Gettysburg Foundation, and used resources of the organization, including attending a seminar at the national park on the defenders of Pickett's Charge.

Writing a book on the Battle of Gettysburg was a daunting task. I needed a lot of assistance to complete this book. As with my other books on history, I found great help from staff members at various research libraries and museums throughout the country. I thank all of them for their assistance.

The research facilities I utilized included Gettysburg National Military Park, the Union League of Philadelphia, Chester County Historical Society, Pennsylvania Historical Society, West Chester University and the Freedoms Foundation at Valley Forge, Pennsylvania. Again, the staff at each institution was helpful in finding artifacts, records and books.

Many individuals also offered support and help in the writing of this book. Susan Mahoney, a great student of history who works hard at keeping history alive in Pennsylvania, was an early supporter of the book. She has a great interest in Gettysburg and Union General Alexander Webb, one of the main characters of this work. She has also reviewed sections of this book. Susan works at West Chester University and aided me in securing a loan of university material. Susan reviewed some of initial chapters. Katherine M. Harlan did her usual excellent copyediting work on my entire manuscript.

Ken Woodward, an educator and student of history, took time to review this manuscript. Stephen Marvin of West Chester University also aided in the securing of documents that aided my understanding of Gettysburg.

Greg Cary, a friend of mine for many years who works at PECO in Chester County, introduced me to Melissa Farkouh, curator of the Medal of Honor Grove at Freedoms Foundation, Valley Forge. Greg is a great supporter of the Medal of Honor Grove and Melissa helped me with the research the Medals of Honor winners from Pickett's Charge. Melissa also displayed medals given during the Civil War and allowed me to photograph them.

Jim, a retired Army officer, and Sally Bartlett of Texas were kind enough to discover a Gettysburg book during their travels and send it to me. Tom and Diane Walsh shared the story of Calvin Parker, Diane's relative, who participated in the charge as a member of a Confederate unit.

Bouncing ideas off other writers and having them review sections of copy is always helpful. Author Lisa Loeb was a great help during the hectic writing days of this book and offered many fine suggestions. She also stored and safeguarded backup sections of the manuscript.

I must also thank my parents, Raymond C. Mowday, Jr. and Ruth Mowday, who took me and my brother Barry and sister Bonnie on trips to Gettysburg as a child. As a result my daughters Melissa and Megan spent a lot of time at Gettysburg in subsequent years. I've reviewed the Pickett's Charge section of the battlefield as the manuscript was being finalized during the summer of 2012 with Megan and her husband Ed Taylor, a Civil War student as is his father Bill Taylor. Along on the trip was my grandson William Bruce Taylor and author Lisa Loeb.

In keeping with mentioning family, I should also recognize William Collins, a relative who fought with the 61st New York in the Wheatfield on July 2, 1863, in Gettysburg. His brother, Samuel George Collins, is a direct descendant of mine and he also served in the 61st New York. My grandmother saved articles Samuel George Collins wrote for the *New York Sunday Mercury* and presented them to me when I was a youngster. The articles helped spark my interest in history and journalism. I thank my grandmother, Anna Savage Mowday Jordan.

I have made what seem to be countless trips to Gettysburg during my lifetime. Those visits increased while I did my research. One fine Saturday afternoon I visited the park with renowned artist Karl Kuerner of Chadds Ford, Pennsylvania, and history enthusiast Bruce Jeffrey. As a Gettysburg tribute, Karl painted a portrait of a Union solder and used Bruce as a model. That portrait, *A Sense of History*, is included in this book. The painting is in the collection of Richard A. McLellan. Rich gave permission to use Karl's great artwork.

A high school friend, Greg DePedro, owner of the

Coatesville Flower Shop, introduced me to one of his relatives. That connection proved to be extremely valuable as it led to my reviewing items from the J. Howard Wert Gettysburg Collection™ and The American Heritage and History Virtual Museum, Inc. Wert began collecting items related to the battle of Gettysburg soon after the conclusion of hostilities at Gettysburg. One rainy day in October 2012 I had the privilege and honor of holding Gettysburg items that included weapons, battle flags and parts of uniforms, even the general's star from General Lewis Armistead's uniform. The experience was quite a thrill for me. I thank Betty Lutze and Greg and Dorie DePedro for their help in assisting to acquire illustrations for this book.

Barricade Books, the publisher of this work, and especially publishers Carole Stuart and Suzanne Henry, also need to be acknowledged. They expressed interest in the work as soon as I suggested the topic. Carole and Suzanne worked hard under deadline pressure to make this book a reality for the 150th anniversary of the Battle of Gettysburg.

INTRODUCTION

Writing a book on the Battle of Gettysburg was not on my mind on a clear and hot summer's day several years ago when I visited the historic battlefield. Thousands and thousands of books and articles have been penned on this pivotal engagement of the American Civil War by esteemed historians and authors of all types of backgrounds. During my research, I found someone wrote in the late 1800s that too many books had been written on Gettysburg. Yes, that statement was made more than 100 years ago and only a few decades after the battle. I've found more than one person today who agrees with the statement. I've also discovered a multitude of people looking forward to another work on Gettysburg.

I've visited Gettysburg many times during my life. On that summer's day I visited what is known as the High Water Mark of the Confederacy. Inside the Angle, I stood at the spot where Lewis Armistead, with his hat rammed on his sword, led those remaining Confederates through a break in the Union lines. I remember walking to the stone wall and looking out across the field where Southern soldiers under the leadership of Major General George Pickett and other Confederate officers made their immortal charge.

At that time I'd read a lot about General Robert E. Lee and the reasons why he felt he had to make that charge on the afternoon of July 3, 1863. I knew Confederate General James Longstreet was not in favor of making the charge and reluctantly followed Lee's orders. I knew about the thousands of Southerners marching off from the relative safety of Seminary Ridge to the defended heights of Cemetery Hill. I knew about the deafening artillery duel that preceded Pickett's Charge.

As my mind's eye was attempting to recreate the historic scene, I moved my head slightly to the left and I looked at the location of the famous copse of trees. The trees were the goal of the charge. The Confederate officers wanted their troops to converge on the copse of trees. My gaze shifted to the low stone wall that served as cover for thin line of Union troops defending against Pickett's Charge. Despite the meager defenses, the Union soldiers stood firm against the Confederate attack.

What did I know about those equally brave Northern troops that stood against Pickett's Charge and saved the Union that day? Not as much as I knew about the operation of the Confederate troops. I knew generals George Gordon Meade commanded the Union army and Winfield Scott Hancock was instrumental in the defense. I knew about the desperate clash at the stone wall and the intense and bloody hand-to-hand combat that lasted minutes. I'm sure the fighting seemed like hours to those involved.

Who were the defenders of Pickett's Charge? How did they come to be positioned at the crucial part of the battlefield that afternoon? What did they experience on that hot summer's day so long ago at Gettysburg?

My journey for this book started with a walk towards the Pennsylvania Monument. Many monuments line the walk from the right of the Union defense on Cemetery Ridge to the Pennsylvania Monument. I stopped and read the inscriptions on the various edifices along Hancock Avenue. I was especially interested in the Philadelphia Brigade as those units held the position where General Armistead and his troops breached the Union's defense. The brigade's commanding officer was Brigadier General Alexander Webb, who took charge of the troops just a few days before the epic battle.

General Webb quickly became a focal point of my research. The West Point graduate won a Medal of Honor for his actions during Pickett's Charge. He was an honored member of the Philadelphia Brigade. A likeness of General Webb hangs in the Union League in Philadelphia. According to the Union League promotional material, the organization was founded to suppress the rebellion of the American Civil War and to preserve the Union. During the Civil War and post-war reconstruction, the Union League was one of the most influential organizations of the North.

I obtained my own image of General Webb at an antique show in suburban Philadelphia. As I walked the rows of dealers, I saw the general's image in a glass case. I pointed to the photograph displayed among a number of other Civil War soldiers. The dealer took the image from the case and handed it to me. I had a chance to handle the picture of one of the heroes of the Battle of Gettysburg. By the end of the two-day show, I struck a deal with the dealer for the image. It's used in this book.

One of my first tasks was to find out what had been

written about the defense of Pickett's Charge. I was told by one of the Gettysburg National Military Park's rangers that information had been written about the Union soldiers on Cemetery Hill. Indeed, that was true. A little information is contained in most books about Pickett's Charge. Those books, inevitably, concentrated on the Southern part of the charge. Most books seemed to devote 80 percent or more of the pages on the planning, organization and execution of orders by Confederate General Robert E. Lee. I also attended a one-day conference sponsored by the Gettysburg Foundation on defending Pickett's Charge. The conference was excellent but more than half of the time was devoted to those making the charge and not on the defenders.

I became convinced that a book on the Union defenders was viable and would contribute something to the understanding of the Battle of Gettysburg. The purpose of this book is to present a narrative about the Union defenders. This book was not intended to review and repeat details of the Confederate planning and execution of Pickett's Charge. They are not contained in this book but are easily obtainable in other publications.

The research of this book took years to complete. I made my way through thousands and thousands of pages of records, letters, official reports and other written documents. During the research I clearly found that historians and others studying the battle have different opinions as to what took place during the afternoon of July 3, 1863. The exact number of troops involved in Pickett's Charge has been debated as has been the exact number of casualties. As with my other books on American history, if I'm unsure of a point I'll inform the reader. I've sought out Gettysburg experts to check the manuscript for accuracy. Eyewitness accounts, especially from those in the midst of fighting, can be misleading. Because of stress and a narrow view of the battle, individual participants' accounts need to be evaluated. I'm sure the debate on what exactly happened during Pickett's Charge will continue.

I utilized as many primary sources as I could for this book. I have quoted from the Official Records of the War of the Rebellion and the John Badger Bachelder papers contained at the Gettysburg National Military Park. The ORs, as the records are known, contain official reports from officers involved in the Civil War. Bachelder, a portrait and landscape painter, collected a number of documents on Gettysburg, beginning just days after the battle and was instrumental in preserving the battlefield. He served from 1883 to 1887 as Superintendent of Tablets and Legends for the Gettysburg Battlefield Memorial Association.

As I have talked about this book to people during my travels and during my talks on historic subjects, I've become aware of the interest Gettysburg has for many people. Not everyone interested in Gettysburg is an expert. Some people get important details wrong, despite the volumes of research. I'm also convinced many people misunderstand Lee's reasoning behind the frontal charge by Longstreet's troops. That charge is known as Pickett's Charge. The attack was far from a suicidal act of insanity, as is a common belief. Lee had no viable option that day other than attacking Meade. Lee devised a plan that might have succeeded if properly executed. Even with all of the mistakes in implementing Lee's plan, the Union line was pierced and almost broken. If General Armistead had been reinforced when he punctured the Union line, the Union army might have retreated in disarray towards Washington. A diplomatic end to the war would then have been possible.

Of course, the draw of Gettysburg is as strong for the descendants of Southern soldiers as Northern ones. During one of my history talks in West Chester, Pennsylvania, I mentioned that I was writing a book on Pickett's Charge. Tom and Dianne Walsh were in the audience and Diane gave me details of her great-great grandfather Calvin Parker's involvement at Gettysburg. Parker was a veteran of Company I, 1st Virginia in Kemper's Brigade. The unit was known as William's Rifles. Parker was wounded three times during the war, the last wound received during Pickett's Charge.

During Picket's Charge, according to information in the Museum of the Confederacy in Richmond, Virginia, Parker tried three times to recapture the company's lost colors and on the third try was wounded in the leg. He suffered on the Gettysburg battlefield all day as the fighting raged around him. He was picked up that evening by Union troops, who, finding him still alive, took him to a hospital tent. There, a surgeon removed his shattered left leg below the knee. For the rest of his life he used a wooden leg. For his extreme bravery in battle, he was awarded a promotion to sergeant major.

More than one person I have talked with has confused

Pickett's Charge with the previous day's fighting on Little Round Top. As the 20th Maine under the direction of Colonel Joshua Lawrence Chamberlain fought valiantly at Little Round Top, so did General Alexander Webb and the Philadelphia Brigade at the Angle defending against Pickett's Charge. Indeed, the Union troops were awarded numerous Medals of Honor for their bravery on the afternoon of July 3, 1863.

Without the heroics of individual officers and enlisted men of the Philadelphia Brigade the other Union units fighting on Cemetery Hill, Lee's forces would have broken Meade's defense, the safety of Washington would have been threatened and the South would have had an excellent opportunity of winning the war. During one of my early research sessions at the research library at Gettysburg National Military Park, park historian and librarian John Heiser said he believed the quick actions of the Union's line officers saved the day for the North. After doing the research for this book I agree with John's assessment.

Pickett's Charge: The Untold Story is one of the least told stories of the epic battle of Gettysburg. The bravery and sense of honor and duty showed by the Union troops matched that of the Southern troops on that hot July day on the farm fields surrounding the community of Gettysburg.

Bruce E. Mowday
West Chester, PA
October 2012

Chapter 1

SEEKING A CONFEDERATE BULLET

F OR SEVERAL BRIEF moments Union General Alexander Stewart Webb had but one thought in his mind on the hot and humid afternoon of July 3, 1863, as he watched brave and gallant Confederate General Lewis Armistead leading his Southern troops as part of the now famous Pickett's Charge.

Armistead, with his hat thrust on the blade of his sword, led the advance of the Rebel's final attempt to rout Union General George Gordon Meade's army at Gettysburg. As the Confederate soldiers breached Webb's defensive position on Cemetery Ridge and rushed into the area that is now known as the High Water Mark of the Confederacy, Webb's one wish was for a Rebel bullet to find a vital part of his body and end his life.

A proud graduate of West Point, 28-year-old General Webb commanded Second Brigade, Second Division of the corps, known as the Philadelphia Brigade. His unit held the strategic defensive point in the Union line. The Philadelphia Brigade was part of General John Gibbon's Second Corps. Gibbon began the campaign in command of the Second Division of the Second Corps and took over temporary command of the Second Corps when General Winfield Scott Hancock was called upon by Meade to manage a larger segment of the Union army that very morning, which included the line on Cemetery Ridge held by the Second, First and Third Corps.

As the Confederate soldiers steadily advanced across Pennsylvania farmland and through the withering fire of Union weapons, generals Gibbon and Webb became keenly aware that their troops would be the key to defeating Pickett's Charge. The outcome of commanding Confederate General Robert E. Lee's invasion of Pennsylvania would depend on the fight in the Union troops and their leadership. The night before Pickett's Charge Meade and his generals predicted Gibbon's section of the Union line would be Lee's target on July 3. Lee had tried breaking both flanks of Meade's defenses during the previous day's fighting at Gettysburg. The Southern troops had come close but failed to dislodge the stubborn Union troops. On the evening of July 2, the strength of the center of the Union line was tested at a certain degree but not to the extent it would be tested on the afternoon of July 3.

The outcome of the Civil War would possibly be determined by the ability of Webb's Philadelphia Brigade and others in the Union's Second Corps to stop those determined Confederate troops advancing upon their position on Cemetery Ridge. General Lee's frontal attack on the Union defenders that day was designed to break the Union line, force the Union army to retreat in disarray and clear the road to Washington, D.C., and President Abraham Lincoln. By putting Washington in peril, the South hoped to enlist the support of European nations.

Lee was convinced victory at Gettysburg was within his grasp as the day dawned on July 3. Lee had little choice but to challenge and defeat Meade's army that day. A withdrawal from Gettysburg and Pennsylvania would be the same as a defeat on the field of battle. Lee couldn't withdraw and dishonor the lives lost in the Southern cause.

If Lee's plan succeeded, the South was in a position to win the Civil War or at least bring about a negotiated settlement to the hostilities. A decisive Southern victory on Northern soil in Pennsylvania could well have broken the will of the Northern populace to continue the bloody war. Some northerners were showing signs they were weary of the war and all of the hardships caused by the fighting. A Confederate victory at Gettysburg would mean Washington, D.C., would be in jeopardy of being seized, or at least threatened, by Lee's army. Lee would still have to face thousands of Union troops if he wanted to capture Washington. The Confederacy would be in a position to receive the international recognition the fledgling country sought and needed to survive.

During the first two days of fighting at Gettysburg, General Lee came close but failed to break the defenses of General Meade. Lee was convinced his plan of attack on the third day of the epic battle, with Pickett's Charge being the centerpiece, would be decisive. Lee planned to launch attacks on several portions of the Union's defensive line. He would re-engage the Northern defenders on Culp's Hill and send General Jeb Stuart's recently arrived cavalry to the rear of the Union army to guard the left flank of the Confederate army and possibly attack when Pickett's forces drove the Union soldiers from the field.

From General Webb's point of view during the midst of the third day's battle, General Lee had good reason to believe the strategy would succeed. At critical moments Webb saw some of the units in his brigade suffer heavy losses and others fail to respond to his order to advance to a stone wall, a forward defensive position, to stop the Confederates.

"When they came over the fences the Army of the Potomac was nearer being whipped than it was at any time of the battle," General Webb wrote. "When my men fell back I almost wished to get killed. I was almost disgraced."[1]

Webb's perceived disgrace centered on his decision to move a section of Battery A, 4th U.S. Artillery commanded by Lieutenant Alonzo Cushing to the stone wall where the Confederate breakthrough took place. Webb second-guessed himself. In the instant when General Armistead vaulted the stone wall, General Webb was convinced he should have sent his infantry, not Cushing's artillery, to the wall to drive back the Confederates.

"I had felt that where I had put Cushing I should have gone myself and wanted the support to take the place where I had placed him,"[2] Webb wrote. For a moment, General Webb believed he was about to be personally responsible for a Union defeat at Gettysburg and maybe for the loss of the whole Civil War.

General Webb desperately wanted a Confederate bullet

to find its mark. Just days after the battle, he wrote to his wife Anna about his wish for death.

✻ ✻ ✻

On February 15, 1835, Alexander Stewart Webb was born in New York City. Webb's family roots have been traced to Gloucestershire, England. Serving in the military was a tradition in his family. Alexander S. Webb's grandfather was Samuel Blatchley Webb, who was wounded in the American Revolution Battle of Bunker Hill while leading a company of light infantry. He received a commendation for bravery. Later in the war Samuel Webb served as aide de camp for General Israel Putnam and in June 1775 he joined the staff of General George Washington. Samuel Webb was made a lieutenant colonel and served as Washington's aide and private secretary.

Samuel Webb was repeatedly wounded as he took part in the battles of Long Island, White Plains and Trenton. Besides his wounds, Webb suffered as a prisoner of war after the British captured him during a raid on Long Island.

Samuel Webb was born in Hartford County, Connecticut, on December 15, 1753, and died on December 3, 1807, in New York. He was the stepson of Continental Congressman and diplomat Silas Deane. Samuel Webb served as Deane's private secretary. After the war Webb was a founder of the Society of the Cincinnati and resided in New York City until becoming a farmer in Claverack. Samuel Webb officiated as Grand Marshal of the Day for Washington's inauguration as the first President of the United States.

There is a historical dispute concerning Webb's holding the Bible for Washington but family history states Samuel Webb, in deed, held the Bible when Washington took the oath of office. Webb's second wife was Caty Hogeboom and they were the parents of James Watson Webb, father of Alexander S. Webb.

James Watson Webb entered the United States Army in 1819 and became a first lieutenant in 1823. He resigned from the army in 1827. James Webb moved to New York City and married Helen Bache Lispenard Stewart, Alexander Webb's mother. Helen Webb died in 1848 and James Webb later married Laura Virginia Cram.

The Webb family was prominent in New York City society as James Webb was a newspaper publisher. James Webb first purchased the *Morning Courier* and then added the *New York Enquirer*. The two publications were merged and the newspaper was titled the *New York Courier and Enquirer*. James Webb was involved with the newspaper for more than three decades. Also, James Webb was a diplomat, serving in both the Abraham Lincoln and Andrew Johnson administrations. He was named minister to Brazil in 1861.

Young Alexander's early schooling was in private schools before he continued in his family's military tradition. He entered the United States Military Academy at West Point in 1851 and graduated in 1855. He was ranked 13 out of the 34 officers in the class and was appointed brevet second lieutenant of artillery.

The year he graduated from West Point he married 23-year-old Anna Elizabeth Remsen. They were wed on

November 28, 1855. The marriage produced eight children. Their eldest daughter Helen Webb Alexandere was born in 1860 as the Civil War was about to begin. She married John E. Alexandere, who was part owner of the Alexander Steamship Lines. Another daughter, Anne Remsen Webb, lived until July 11, 1943.

Webb's first assignment as a second lieutenant was with the 4th United States Artillery. Webb was sent to Florida to take part in the Seminole War. He saw action in 1856. Upon completion of duty in Florida, Webb spent time in 1856 and 1857 on garrison duty at Fort Independence and later Fort Snelling. Fort Independence guarded the harbor of Boston, Massachusetts, while Fort Snelling was located near St. Paul, Minnesota.

Webb returned to West Point in November 1857 when he was appointed assistant professor of mathematics. Many of the cadets he tutored would see action as officers in the upcoming Civil War. He remained at his appointed post at West Point until January 1861 when he resigned his position. The nation, both North and South, was preparing for war.

The inaugural parade for newly elected President Abraham Lincoln included Webb. On Monday, March 4, 1861, Lincoln addressed the nation in his first inaugural address and made his position clear that secession would not be tolerated. Lincoln promised to defend all government property and places, which included Fort Sumter.

Webb's assignment in the nation's capital concluded on April 4, 1861. Nine days later troops under the command of Confederate General Pierre Gustave Toutant

Beauregard fired upon Union-held Fort Sumter in the harbor of Charleston, South Carolina. The great American Civil War formally commenced.

After departing Washington Webb's first stop was at Fort Pickens at Pensacola Bay, Florida. His promotion to first lieutenant came on April 28, 1861. Fort Pickens, named for Revolutionary War hero Andrew Pickens, was one of only four forts in the South that were never occupied by Confederate forces during the Civil War.

Webb's time spent in Florida was brief as he was ordered to join the Army of Northeastern Virginia, as it was then named, under the command of General Irvin McDowell. Webb was promoted to captain of the 11th United States Infantry and was present when McDowell's forces were routed by Confederate General Beauregard's army at the First Battle of Bull Run on July 21, 1861.

Elements of McDowell's army retreated in disarray to Washington after the loss of Bull Run. Panic spread through the civilian population as the Confederate forces were within easy striking distance of the city. As the Lincoln administration worked to secure Washington, Webb's assignment was to be assistant to General William F. Barry, chief of artillery of the Army of the Potomac. For the next six months, Webb took part in defending Washington.

General Barry wrote of Webb, "He rendered me that intelligent, faithful and energetic assistance that gave promise of the still greater soldierly qualities that distinguished him later in the war."[3]

Webb's next promotion was to major of the 1ˢᵗ Rhode Island Artillery Volunteers in September 1861.

Major Webb took part in the Peninsula campaign under General George B. McClellan. McClellan, known as the "Young Napoleon," was officially put in charge of the Federal army on July 27, 1861, and given the task of making the mostly volunteer army a professional fighting force. Over time President Abraham Lincoln became convinced that McClellan was not America's Napoleon.

President Lincoln was anxious for McClellan to engage the Confederate army and finally, in March 1862, McClellan began the Peninsular campaign. McClellan's strategy was to take Richmond, Virginia, the capital of the Confederacy, by first transporting his troops by water to within striking distance of Richmond.

On March 17, 1862, McClellan moved twelve divisions of his Army of the Potomac to Fort Monroe near Hampton, Virginia. Webb was among the troops that passed through Fort Monroe to fight in the Peninsula campaign. Richmond was 80 miles to the west of Fort Monroe and McClellan's forces pressed the Confederates and threatened Richmond.

Confederate victories under General Joseph Eggleston Johnston and later the newly appointed commander of the army Robert E. Lee, drove McClellan's forces back to the James River and thus ended Union hopes of quickly ending the war by taking Richmond. Lee assumed command of the army, defending Richmond on June 1 after Johnston was twice wounded at the battle of Seven Pines. Webb took part in the battles at Yorktown, Mechanicsville and Gaines' Mill during the campaign.

Another promotion was in the offing for Webb as he became lieutenant colonel of volunteers on August 20, 1862, and served as chief of staff in General Fitz John Porter's V Corps during the campaign in Maryland, which included the pivotal battle of Antietam. Lee's first attempt to invade the North was thwarted at Antietam on September 17, 1862. The next night Lee's army retreated back into Virginia.

After Antietam, Webb was once again assigned to Washington and served as Inspector of Artillery until January 1863, when he returned to the Army of the Potomac as assistant inspector general of General George G. Meade's V Corps.

Webb's time as a staff officer was about to conclude. Within months he would be commanding troops in the field.

General Joseph Hooker was in command of the Army of the Potomac during the battle of Chancellorsville in May 1863. Hooker, even though his army was larger than Lee's Confederate forces, was defeated in a battle that many consider Lee's masterpiece of strategy. Lee's victory came at a steep price as Confederate General Thomas "Stonewall" Jackson, Lee's ablest and most dependable general, suffered a wound by friendly fire that led to first the loss of his arm and then to the loss of his life.

In the midst of the hectic and confusing fight at Chancellorsville on May 3, 1863, Meade needed an officer to take over a detachment of his corps. Meade selected Webb. In

Meade's report after the battle Meade called "particular attention" to Webb's "intelligence and zeal" [4] during the fight.

General Meade and young officer Alexander S. Webb were united when they began their march to destiny at Gettysburg.

Chapter 2

PRELUDE TO GETTYSBURG

THE DISHEARTENING DEFEAT at Chancellorsville gave President Lincoln pause. Once again Lincoln questioned the top leadership of the Army of the Potomac. Since the beginning of the war, Lincoln tried and failed numerous times to find a general he believed could quell the rebellion. General Joseph Hooker, who led the army at Chancellorsville, obviously wasn't the general to save the Union.

The defeat at Chancellorsville gave Confederate General Robert E. Lee a perfect opportunity to invade the North. A campaign in the Northern states would give the populace of the Confederacy in Virginia a break from the ravages of the war. Also, the Northern farmers would have to feed the armies, giving the Southern farmers a much needed respite. Lee was determined to defeat the Union army on its own turf and force a conclusion to the Civil War. Soon after the victory at Chancellorsville, Lee was on the road to Gettysburg and destiny.

Major command changes in the Army of Potomac took place in the days preceding Gettysburg, the pivotal battle of the Civil War. Some Union officers, soldiers and government officials didn't have faith in the generals of their army. A string of embarrassing losses instilled distrust. From the perspective of many Union soldiers, the invasion of the

North was another disaster in the making. Lincoln making another leadership change didn't increase confidence.

The rippling effects of the reorganization of the Army of the Potomac resulted in Lieutenant Colonel Alexander S. Webb being placed in a position that would affect the outcome of Gettysburg and the future of the United States of America.

Webb began the march to Gettysburg on the staff of General George Gordon Meade. A week before the first shots were fired at Gettysburg, Webb was promoted to brigadier general of volunteers. The newly minted general would have only three days to gain the respect of his new command, the Philadelphia Brigade. The brigade was comprised of four units, the 69th Pennsylvania, 71st Pennsylvania, 72nd Pennsylvania and the 106th Pennsylvania volunteers. The brigade was not about to welcome a new leader with open arms. They were content with General Joshua Thomas "Paddy" Owen, their commander. Owen had led the brigade, including the 69th Pennsylvania that was composed mostly of Irish soldiers from Philadelphia, Pennsylvania.

One author contended, "When the men of the 69th (Pennsylvania) first laid their eyes on their new brigade commander, they held their tongues. Here was a man without any combat experience who dressed like a dandy. A man who openly talked and wrote about his disrespect for the Irish soldier. A man who had already decided to be a harsh disciplinarian with his new brigade."[5]

The leadership position of the Philadelphia Brigade came

open after Brigadier General John Gibbon, commander of the Second Division of the Second Corps of the Army of the Potomac, placed Owen under arrest.

Owen was born on March 29, 1821, in Cammarthen, Wales, and came to the United States as a youth and settled in the Chestnut Hill area of Philadelphia. He helped establish the Chestnut Hill Academy for Boys along with his brother. Owen joined the army in May 1861 and became colonel of the 69th Pennsylvania in August of the same year. His promotion to brigadier general came in November 1862.

Official records are devoid of the reasons Gibbon had for placing Owen under arrest. Speculation centered on Owen's alcohol consumption. Owen also had a reputation for being a lax disciplinarian. His unit had too many stragglers during marches for Gibbon's liking. Desertions were common in Owen's command as were arrests for numerous petty and serious offenses. One shooting incident between two officers was recorded where a captain was killed. Captain Bernard McMahon of the 71st Pennsylvania was charged and convicted of the May 27, 1863, murder of Captain Andrew McManus of E Company of the 69th Pennsylvania.

Colonel Dennis O'Kane, also of the 69th Pennsylvania, had his own issues with Owen and the commander's drinking. In October 1862 at Harpers Ferry, O'Kane's family, including his wife and oldest daughter, visited him. O'Kane's family was taking a carriage ride when an intoxicated Owen approached them on horseback. Owen rode his mount several times into the carriage and then invited O'Kane's daughter to spend the night in his tent.

O'Kane dismounted, grabbed Owen, his commanding officer, and pulled Owen from his horse. O'Kane recalled Owen's head bounced when it hit the ground. O'Kane was charged for the assault on Owen but acquitted at a court martial. Owen was also charged for his misconduct, convicted and sentenced to dismissal from the service. Owen was then reinstated due to political intervention from Owen supporters in Pennsylvania.[6]

Gary Lash's history of the 71st Pennsylvania, also known as the California Regiment, noted, "All things considered, the men had little to complain of on Bull Run Mountain until John Gibbon placed General Owen under arrest. The division commander appears to have held a strong dislike for Owen, though the latter's offense remains puzzling. From all appearances, the Philadelphia Brigade had behaved reasonably well to this point of the march north. Perhaps Gibbon held little regard for a man whom he believed had risen to the rank of brigadier general through little more than political means."[7]

Gibbon wanted an officer who could impose order and discipline in the brigade. His selection was General Alexander S. Webb.

❊ ❊ ❊

One of the people responsible for the forming of the Philadelphia Brigade in the summer of 1861 was Edward Dickinson Baker. Baker was a lawyer, United States Senator from Oregon, a former member of the United States House of Representatives from Illinois and a close personal friend of President Lincoln.

Baker served in the United States Army as a colonel during the war with Mexico. He practiced law for almost a decade in San Francisco before the Civil War began. Baker also worked hard in California and Oregon to help secure Lincoln's election in 1860. Lincoln even named his son Edward after Baker.[8]

When the Civil War began, Northern states were required to raise a specific number of troops. Senator Baker was authorized to form a regiment that was to be credited to the quota of troops to be raised by California. Most of Baker's recruiting was done in the Philadelphia area. Baker became colonel of the 71st Pennsylvania in June 1861 and the unit was also known as the 1st California. He was offered a general's rank but declined. If Baker would have accepted the commission, he would have had to resign from the Senate. He was allowed to remain a Senator being a colonel of the volunteers.

On October 20, 1861, Baker visited with Lincoln on the lawn of the White House. "It was a golden autumn day and leaves and foliage were ablaze with colors. Willie (Lincoln's young son) played in some leaves nearby, calling out from time to time for his father and Baker to watch. Lincoln leaned against a tree and Baker stretched out on the grass, both of them talking earnestly about the war."[9]

Lincoln and Baker spoke of the next day's military operation. Baker was eager to take part in the planned fight under the command of General George B. McClellan, the first of Lincoln's commanders of the Army of the Potomac.

On the day after his visit with President Lincoln, on October 21, 1861, Baker was killed at the Battle of Ball's Bluff, Virginia. He was the only sitting United States Senator to be killed in action in the war. Lincoln was reported to be visibly upset when told of his friend's death. "Lincoln left the office with his hands pressed hard against his chest, stumbled when he stepped out into the street, and returned to the White House without a word to anyone."[10]

* * *

After Baker's death the California references to the brigade disappeared and General William Wallace Burns was given command of the Philadelphia Brigade. About this time, in November 1862, General Ambrose Burnside replaced McClellan as commander of the Army of the Potomac. The Philadelphia Brigade received a new leader, Paddy Owen.

Lash's article on The Philadelphia Brigade at Gettysburg in the July issue of *Gettysburg Magazine* notes that the 72nd Pennsylvania was recruited by DeWitt Clinton Baxter from mostly fire companies in Philadelphia in August 1861 and was at first called Baxter's Fire Zouaves. They wore distinctive uniforms that included wide-cut, light-blue pants with red stripes, a cut-away jacket and rows of bright buttons. A bright shirt would include insignias of the soldier's fire department. A regulation cap and white leggings completed the uniform. Lash indicated the uniform was worn at Gettysburg but gave way to the standard Union uniform. The previous hard campaigning took a toll on the original uniform.

On June 2, 1863, incidents in Washington and in the field contributed to the reorganization of the leadership of the Philadelphia Brigade. President Lincoln met with General John F. Reynolds of Pennsylvania about taking over for General Hooker. Reynolds, recognized as one of the best officers in the Union army, was not elevated to overall command of the Army of the Potomac. Reynolds reportedly wouldn't accept the promotion until he had total control over the army. On July 1, 1863, Reynolds would become the first general killed at Gettysburg in fighting west of the town. In the camp of the Philadelphia Brigade on June 2, two desertions were reported. Paddy Owen's reputation as a lax disciplinarian was reinforced in Gibbon's eyes.

General Lee was not wasting time celebrating after the Chancellorsville victory. On June 3, 1863, a portion of the Confederate army departed the Fredericksburg, Virginia, area and headed west. A section of General James Longstreet's corps led the way. The march to Gettysburg had begun. The next day General Richard Ewell's corps followed Longstreet's men. Only Confederates under the command of General A. P. Hill remained in the Fredericksburg vicinity.

Union General Hooker was aware Lee's army was shifting position but he failed to attack Hill's corps, even though he had a superior force. Hooker instead concentrated on trying to determine the destination of Lee's army.

On June 8 Lee was at Culpeper Court House, Virginia, with the men under the command of Longstreet and Ewell. General James Ewell Brown (Jeb) Stuart's cavalry was also on the scene. The next day Stuart's command was attacked by Union cavalry at Brandy Station. The engagement has been touted by some as the greatest cavalry battle ever in America. Stuart held the field at the conclusion of the fighting but the Union cavalry forces under General Alfred Pleasonton fought well. Pleasonton also discovered that Confederate infantry was located west of Fredericksburg.

As Lee continued his march to the north, Hooker asked permission to launch a campaign against Richmond, Virginia. President Lincoln ordered Hooker to concentrate on defeating Lee's army and protecting Washington, D.C. Hooker was not to advance on Richmond and capture the capital city of the Confederacy. Lincoln was intent on protecting the Northern states and their populace. Lincoln also knew that until Lee's army was defeated, the Confederacy would live.

Lee's forces made their way to the vicinity of Winchester, Virginia, and attacked Union forces under General Robert H. Milroy. Milroy decided to withdraw from Winchester during the early morning hours of June 15 but the Confederates had blocked his route to safety. Milroy reported losses of about 4,000 men, 23 field guns, 300 wagons, 300 horses and large quantities of commissary and quartermasters' stores. The first engagement on the road to Gettysburg was a Southern victory.

The overwhelming victory bolstered Confederate spirits

as the march continued to Northern soil. Also, A. P. Hill's forces were on the move to join the rest of the Southern army. By mid-June, the threat of invasion was clear. Hooker told Lincoln, "It is not in my power to prevent an invasion."[11] Some of the citizens of Harrisburg were ready to flee the capital city of the Commonwealth of Pennsylvania in fear of a Confederate invasion, according to newspaper reports of the time.

General Hooker became mired in a strategy dispute with General Henry Halleck, Lincoln's chief military advisor and commander in chief of all Union troops from 1862 until March 1864. Hooker was of a mind to force a confrontation with Lee to the north of Washington while Halleck wanted Hooker to stay on Lee's heels and secure the federal arsenal at Harpers Ferry. Hooker feared he had lost the confidence of Halleck and appealed directly to Lincoln for assistance and guidance. Lincoln rebuffed Hooker. Hooker was ordered to follow the orders of Halleck.

Members of the 71st Pennsylvania of the Philadelphia Brigade reported the Gettysburg campaign started for them on June 17. The regiment was part of action at Thoroughfare Gap. The unit was attacked by Confederates and a two-hour skirmish took place. After repulsing the attack, Colonel Richard Penn Smith's regiment, the 71st Pennsylvania, was ordered to a position where he could observe the enemy and blockade a road to prevent another enemy attack on the main body of the army. Smith discovered the enemy about three miles from the Second Corps. Smith's soldiers felled trees across the road making it impassable.

The threat to the Second Corps was thwarted by the members of the Philadelphia Brigade.

*　*　*

Colonel Smith wrote about the march to Gettysburg in a letter dated July 29, 1863, to General Isaac Jones Wistar. "Our march from Falmouth (June 15) until this hour has been attended with many privations—hardships and danger. Our march has been constant—long and fatiguing, 20 miles per day is considered by us now as a walk. As wagon guard, I marched 34 miles one day, in all I did not rest one hour, in order I was complimented. . . . In the marching from Dumfries to Wolf Run shores, I had but one straggler. . . . You are doubtless anxious to know and hear of our chase after Gen'l Lee. Suffice to say that we made forced marches day and night til we overtook him. For a week at a time we have not seen our wagons. And our sufferings have been many for an army. Though I stood the campaign well, I assure you I suffered much by it. At times deadly sick."[12]

Lieutenant Colonel Charles H. Morgan, inspector general and chief of staff for General Winfield Hancock, issued a report on the early stages of the march. The report is contained in the Bachelder Papers of the National Park Service, Gettysburg. "On the night of the 13th (June) and morning of the 14th the Second Corps, following the track of the 6th (Corps), moved from Falmouth, reaching Stafford (Court House) some time after daylight. The Court House was in flames having been fired by some of the stragglers from the preceding column. Resting here for two or three hours, we moved on towards Dumfries as far as Aquia Creek (northern Virginia), where we went into camp for the night. The day was intensely hot and the roads were dusty which rendered the march one of great fatigue to the men. Several hundred of them fell out. Numerous cases of sun-stroke occurred and all the ambulances in the corps were sent back to assist in getting in the men. The commander of the guard denied permission to fire a few shots of artillery toward the mass of stragglers to give them the impression that the enemy were following."[13]

* * *

Those Northern residents in the path of the invading army took precautions to protect themselves from the Confederate army. On Saturday, June 20, 1863, "in Baltimore breastworks were being erected north and west of the city as a precaution against Confederate raids. At Shippensburg, Penn., the owner of the Union Hotel blurred his sign with brown paint."[14] On June 22 skirmishes were reported to have taken place on Pennsylvania soil. Two days later at Sharpsburg, Maryland, site of the battle of Antietam the previous September, fighting again took place.

In the early morning hours of June 25, Jeb Stuart departed from Salem Depot, Virginia, to pass between the armies of Lee and Hooker. Stuart was to rejoin Lee's army north of the Potomac River. Lee had given Stuart permission for the operation but didn't expect Stuart to be out of touch with Lee for a week. Lee's orders were not specific. Stuart would not rejoin Lee's army until July 2, too late to help Lee plan and execute his Gettysburg battle plans. Stuart and his troops would participate in the fighting on July 3, 1863.

Pennsylvania Governor Andrew Curtin was worried about the safety of his constituents and on June 26 Curtin called for 60,000 volunteers to serve three months and aid in driving Lee from the Commonwealth. Curtin had good reason to fret as Lee and commands of Hill and Longstreet were in Pennsylvania and causing turmoil. General Early accepted the surrender of undefended York, Pennsylvania. The next scheduled stop for Early's troops was the seizing of bridges across the Susquehanna River.

As Governor Curtin was desperately looking for men to defend Pennsylvania, President Lincoln decided the time had come for a change in leadership of the Army of Potomac. General Hooker continued to disagree and question the Lincoln Administration's strategy on defending Harpers Ferry and engaging Lee's army.

Confederate General Early was seeking supplies and money from Pennsylvania towns. At York he departed with $28,600 and some needed material for his troops.

General Hooker wrote a letter on June 27 to General Henry W. Halleck, general-in-chief of the Union armies concerning the defense of Harpers Ferry. Hooker contended the public property was secured, the arsenal safe from attack and the 10,000 troops ready for service in the field. Hooker wanted his message relayed to the "Secretary of War and His Excellency the President."[15] Hooker continued, "My original instructions require me to cover

Harpers Ferry and Washington. I have now imposed upon me, in addition, an enemy in my front of more than my number. I beg to be understood, respectfully, but firmly, that I am unable to comply with this condition with the means at my disposal, and earnestly request that I may at once be relieved from the position I occupy."

Halleck replied to Hooker at 8:00 p.m. on June 27. The order read, "Your application to be relieved from your present command is received. As you were appointed to this command by the President, I have no power to relieve you. Your dispatch has been duly referred for Executive action."[16]

A change in command of Union forces was clearly in the offing. Meade's name was prominent despite a somewhat cool lunch meeting between Meade and Lincoln as Meade thought Lincoln "indifferent." Meade's sister Margaret worked in the War Department and believed Meade was in line for the promotion. Meade's wife Margaretta Sergeant Meade warned her husband, "Do not accept, it would only be your ruin."[17]

On June 27 Lincoln settled on General George Gordon Meade to be the general in charge of the Army of the Potomac. Halleck wrote Meade, "You will receive with this the order of the President placing you in command of the Army of the Potomac. Considering the circumstances, no one ever received a more important command; and I cannot doubt that you will fully justify the confidence, which the Government has reposed in you."[18]

Meade, born in Spain of American parents, graduated from West Point in 1835. An engineer, he left the army to pursue a civilian career but rejoined the army to fight in Mexico. General Ulysses S. Grant wrote of Meade, "He was brave and conscientious, and commanded the respect of all who knew him. He was unfortunately of a temper that would get beyond his control at times."[19]

At 7:00 a.m. on Sunday, June 28, Meade was in Frederick, Maryland, when he received General Hallack's order placing him in charge of the Army of the Potomac. He issued a reply. Meade commented that his elevation in command was a surprise and he didn't even know where his troops were positioned, let alone the position of the enemy.

General Meade would have little time to figure out the situation. Within a week, Meade would fight the pivotal battle of the Civil War at Gettysburg. Meade's first move was towards the Susquehanna River so he could defend both Baltimore and Washington and be in position to engage Lee's army.

When Lee learned of Meade's movements, he ordered his top commanders, Longstreet, Hill and Ewell, to move in the direction of Cashtown, Pennsylvania, near Gettysburg, and Meade. The order meant the immediate Confederate threat against Harrisburg no longer existed. Early's troops and other Confederate units halted within striking distance of Harrisburg and started to retrace their path. Early was heading south towards the little town of Gettysburg.

* * *

General Alexander S. Webb took command of the Philadelphia Brigade at 5:00 p.m. on Sunday, June 28, 1863, just ten hours after Meade took command of the Army of the Potomac. The two Union officers faced difficult circumstances and made crucial decisions during the next week. Webb, a non-Irishman, had to quickly gain the respect of his troops and impose some military discipline. Webb was a proud West Point graduate and viewed as a no-nonsense officer. He was described as being a handsome man with a compact build, bronzed complexion, dark hair and a goatee. Colonel Charles Wainwright described Webb as being conscientious, hard working and fearless. Wainwright was a friend and described many of his conversations with Webb on the road to Gettysburg. An aide of Meade, Theodore Lyman, commented that Webb was jolly, pleasant and paid attention to details. Webb also had an unnerving habit of laughing in a convulsive manner, according to Lyman.

First impressions of Webb by members of the 71st Pennsylvania were not favorable. "Of more immediate concern to the (members of the former) Californian regiment was the appointment of 28-year-old Alexander Stewart Webb to command of the Philadelphia Brigade, a native New Yorker and graduate of the West Point class of 1855, he was a bit of a dandy. He had fought against the Seminoles in 1856, and, more recently, had taken part in the defense of Fort Pickens and the calamity at First Bull Run, yet the newly minted brigadier had spent much of the war languishing in staff positions.

"Colonel Richard Penn Smith (of the 71st Pennsylvania) described Webb as a `solider and a gentleman' in a letter to fellow officer General Isaac Jones Wistar. Smith went on to say, "The army appears to have more confidence in Gen'l Meade than it did in Gen'l Hooker." The rank and file knew little of their smartly dressed commander. First Lieutenant John Rogers of Company B remembered, 'His dress and personality attracted us the moment we first laid eyes on him." . . . It appears that Webb entered into his new assignment harboring a bit of a grudge against the Philadelphia Brigade for what he believed to be a history of straggling. He was going to change that."[20]

His new command spent the night under his leadership near the Monocacy River, east of Frederick, Maryland. Many in the Philadelphia Brigade didn't know Webb and couldn't recognize their new commanding officer. The lack of familiarity would cause a major problem during a critical point in the defense of Pickett's Charge on July 3.

Webb's first opportunity to impose some discipline in the Philadelphia Brigade came during the first full day of his command. The Second Corps was ordered to move early in the morning. While most the troops of the corps were on the road and marching by 6:00 a.m., the Philadelphia Brigade was late in beginning the 33-mile trek to Uniontown, near the Pennsylvania border. Webb informed his staff officers he intended to catch-up with the rest of the corps by not marching on the main road but by twice crossing the Monocacy River, a tributary of the Potomac River.

At a ford in the river, Webb ordered his soldiers not to halt and to cross the river. Some of the soldiers stopped to take off their shoes and socks before entering the river. To set an example, Webb waded into the water with his high boots. He wanted his troops to keep moving. The personal demonstration by Webb didn't impress the soldiers.

Joseph R. C. Ward's *History of the 106th Pennsylvania* describes the crossing of the Monocacy River. Without a bridge, the troops had to wade across the river. The water covered the men's kneecaps. "Men stopped as they usually did to take off their shoes and stockings and roll up their pants, but General Webb found that was taking too much time and he was anxious to make up for that lost (time), so he ordered the men to wade right in, and jumping from his horse stood in the middle of the stream until the whole Brigade had passed, ordering each man that hesitated to move on at once; of course, this met with the disapproval of the men, who were not backward in expressing their feelings in terms not very complimentary to the General, and the remarks might have been heard by him had he chosen to listen.

"One of the 69th Regiment, more bold than the rest and with his natural Irish bluntness, addressed as he passed: 'Sure it's no wonder ye can stand there when ye are leather up to your waist.' The General having on a pair of long boots that came up above his knees. This created a good laugh by those who heard it; he paid no attention whatever, but continued to order his men forward and remained there until the last man had crossed.

"It was here that Captain Breitenbach of Company G, got himself into trouble by trying to evade those orders of General Webb, meant to apply to officers as well as men, by trying to cross the creek on a log instead of wading. He got halfway cross the creek when seen by the General, who ordered him back and placed him in arrest."[21]

Assistant Surgeon Dr. Daniel McLean gave Breitenbach a letter saying his "pre-disposition to rheumatism rendered his wading through the creek dangerous to his health," according to the history of the regiment. Breitenbach went to General Webb with his medical letter but Webb lectured Breitenbach on disobeying orders. Breitenbach was then released from arrest and returned to duty.

Webb's way of dealing with stragglers appears to have been effective. After complaining to his officers about the situation, Webb "ordered that the officers should arrest any of the men found straggling and to bring them to him and he would shoot them like dogs."[22] The number of those soldiers lagging behind the brigade on marches was quickly reduced.

Webb issued an unpopular order on June 30 that didn't improve his standing within his command. He made his officers resume wearing their officers' insignia on their uniforms. Many of the officers had taken to dressing as privates. By doing so, the officers were less of an inviting target for Confederate sharpshooters. A member of the 71st Pennsylvania recalled Webb saying, "There are few of you whom I am able to recognize as officers, as you have no insignia of office except your swords."[23]

Webb wasn't making friends with any level of his command.

Webb did win over some members of the Philadelphia Brigade. "Brig. Gen. Alexander Webb of the Regular Army assumed command of our Brigade, relieving General Owen. This was another unexpected change, and a man we knew nothing about, but soon found that he was a soldier in the full (definition) of the word."[24]

While Webb was dealing with uniforms and discipline, Meade's army was closing on Gettysburg. Indeed, on Tuesday, June 30, 1863, the advance troopers of General John Buford's cavalry were approaching the town. On the last day of June, Meade approved a request by 42-year-old General John Reynolds to advance to Gettysburg. Lee's Confederates were on their way to confront Reynolds and Buford.

Reynolds, who was born in Pennsylvania at Lancaster, was riding to his death. On July 1, 1863, Reynolds became the first general killed at Gettysburg.

* * *

On the day Reynolds died, General Webb and the Philadelphia Brigade marched within four miles of Gettysburg. The order received by Webb at 3:00 p.m. was to proceed with all haste to Gettysburg. The arrival of the unit on Pennsylvania soil was noted as 5:00 p.m. and by 9:00 p.m. the Philadelphia Brigade halted southeast of the Round Tops.

The brigade was ordered into a position to cover the First Army Corps' retreat, if the Union troops were forced to flee the Gettysburg battlefield.

"On the evening of the first of July (we) arrived at field of Gettysburg. We could hear the heavy artillery fire of the First Corps who were on the advance and later in the day we received the sad intelligence of the death of Gen. Reynolds, which was regarded as a calamity, for his ability as a commander was second to none," according to Private Anthony W. McDermott of Company I, 69th Pennsylvania.[25]

During the evening of the first day of fighting, the Second Corps commanded by General Winfield Scott Hancock made its way to Cemetery Ridge. Hancock played an important role in forming the defensive line that thwarted General Lee's attempts of breaking the Union defense and opening the road to Washington, D.C.

Hancock's report as part of the Official Records of the War of Rebellion stated, "On the morning of July 1, the command marched to Taneytown, going into bivouac about 11 a.m. I then proceeded in person to General Meade's headquarters, and, on reporting to him, was informed as to his intention with reference to giving battle to the enemy, the orders for preparatory movements being then ready for issue.

"A few minutes before 1 p.m., I received orders to proceed in person to the front, and assume command of the First, Third, and Eleventh Corps, in consequence of the death of Major-General Reynolds. Having been fully informed by the major-general commanding as to his intentions, I was instructed by him to give the necessary directions upon my arrival at the front for the movement of troops and trains to the rear toward the line of battle he had selected, should I deem it expedient to do so. If the ground was suitable, and circumstances made it wise, I was directed to establish the line of battle at Gettysburg.

"Turning over the command of the Second Corps to Brigadier-General Gibbon, under instructions from General Meade, at 1:10 o'clock I was on the road to Gettysburg, accompanied by my personal aides, Lieutenant-Colonel Morgan, chief of staff, Second Corps, and the signal party of the corps, under command of Captain Hall.

"At 3 p.m. I arrived at Gettysburg and assumed the command. At this time the First and Eleventh Corps were retiring through the town, closely pursued by the enemy. The cavalry of General Buford was occupying a firm position on the plain to the left of Gettysburg, covering the rear of the retreating troops."[26]

* * *

Early in the morning of July 2, 1863, the Philadelphia Brigade was roused from slumber and made ready to change locations. At 3:00 a.m. they were stirring and they were moving by dawn.

Ward's regimental history noted that the soldiers "marched two miles to a field near Taneytown Road and were addressed by General Webb. He had been with us but three days; the men knew nothing of him, and their experience at the Monocacy Creek had the effect to make him unpopular; but that short address in which he told them that they would now be called upon to defend their own state by hard fighting, that it would require each man to do his full duty to defeat the elated enemy, and appealed to each to cheerfully do his duty, and then told them that any one found shirking it in the slightest degree would be severely dealt with, that he would shoot any one leaving the line, and called on any man to do the same to him if he failed in his duty, told them, that they had a commander that would not fail in his duty nor allow the men to fail in theirs: and when the fight was over they knew that he had proven himself to be all they could expect—one of the bravest officers of the Army."[27]

The members of the Philadelphia Brigade arrived on Cemetery Ridge and were posted near the headquarters of General Meade. First Lieutenant Frank Aretas Haskell of the 6th Wisconsin Infantry and an aide to General Gibbon, wrote that "when Meade arrived on the field he established his headquarters at a shabby little farmhouse on the left of the Taneytown Road, the house nearest the line and a little more than five hundred yards in rear of what became the centre of the position of the Second Corps."[28]

The Philadelphia Brigade troops were placed upon the crest of a ridge, just west of the farmhouse. The 71st Pennsylvania's line was established along a low stone wall near what was to become the now famous angle of the defense of Pickett's Charge.

The 69th Pennsylvania was placed in line, "a little below the crest on the decline facing the enemy and behind a low stone wall, the right resting within about thirty paces of what is now designated as the 'Bloody Angle,' the left extending about the same distance below, or south of a clump of trees of umbrella shape, historically known as the focal point or guide for the rebel Gen. Pickett in his advance and charge of the 3rd of July."[29]

Chapter 3

SECOND DAY AT GETTYSBURG

A S THE MORNING of Thursday, July 2, 1863, progressed, Union General George Meade placed elements of his command into a defense line that stretched from the fringes of the town of Gettysburg to Cemetery Ridge beyond Culp's Hill to Little Round Top. The line resembled a fish hook. During the next 48 hours fierce fighting would take place at all sections of Meade's defense and testing the men of the Army of the Potomac.

Confederate General Robert E. Lee, at the same time, was maneuvering his own troops beyond Seminary Ridge. The ridge, trees and hilly terrain masked the movements from Meade's direct eyesight. Lee's mission at Gettysburg was to drive Meade from the field and force a Union retreat towards Washington, D.C.

Between the two generals was a section of open field that would become the scene of Pickett's Charge on July 3. The units of the Second Corps, including the Philadelphia Brigade, held the main defensive positions. General Alexander Webb's men had hard work before them that Thursday before receiving Pickett's Charge on the following day.

Lee would test the strength of both Union flanks before attacking the middle of the Union line held by the Philadelphia Brigade. The next 36 hours would be a trying time for Webb and his new command. Webb was up to the challenge. His handling of the Philadelphia Brigade led some to conclude Webb's most memorable military service of the Civil War took place at Gettysburg.

* * *

Captain Andrew. H. Embler, acting assistant adjutant-general, received a brief report on the deployment made by division commander General John Gibbon and the early action seen by the Philadelphia Brigade. The right flank was placed next to Battery A of the 4th U.S. Artillery commanded by Lieutenant Alonzo Cushing. Cushing won a Medal of Honor for his service at Gettysburg and he also lost his life. The unit's left flank rested at Battery B of the 1st Rhode Island Artillery. The artillery unit would later be moved in front of the Pennsylvania 69th. The other regiments of the Philadelphia Brigade were massed in support of the artillery.

The 69th Pennsylvania was placed at west side of Cemetery Ridge. The troopers reached their position just after sunrise. Their initial position was just below the crest of a small rise and behind a low stone wall. The unit's position was a few yards from an area that would become known as the "Bloody Angle." The angle was the intersection of two sections of a stone wall. Just to the rear of the unit was a copse of trees, a thicket of small trees and shrubs. The 69th Pennsylvania held the ground that would later be part of what is called the "High Water Mark of the Confederacy."

According to Embler's report, The Pennsylvania 69th regiment was placed behind a fence a little in advance of the

ridge; the remaining three regiments of the brigade under
cover of the hill in rear. Captain John J. Sperry and members of Companies A and I, of the 72nd Pennsylvania and
Companies A and B, of the 106h Pennsylvania were sent to
skirmish and to watch the movements of the enemy. Sperry
lost a number of men and had several officers wounded in
performing this important duty. Embler wrote to Gibbon
that Captains Sperry and James C. Lynch, of the 106th
Pennsylvania and Captains Cook and Suplee, of the 72nd
Pennsylvania deserved honorable mention for their coolness,
intelligence, and zeal shown both on the July 2 and July 3.

* * *

Of the day's activities, General Hancock reported sharp
skirmishing occurred during the morning, particularly in
front of Hays' division. Hays' men captured prisoners. The
artillery was frequently engaged, but no severe fighting took
place until about 3 p.m., when the Third Corps advanced
from its position toward the Emmitsburg Road and became
heavily engaged. Hancock also reported the Fifth Corps
became engaged in the vicinity of Round Top, in support
of and some distance to the rear of the Third Corps.

General Webb and his units waited for orders during the
hot July day but were not further engaged until evening.
Webb had a perfect view of the skirmishing that took place
before his troops during the early afternoon hours of July
2, 1863. While the Philadelphia Brigade waited to be called
action, other elements of the Union army were engaged in
a fierce struggle with Lee's troops.

General Daniel Sickles's handling of his troops put the Union army at severe risk. Sickles, commanding the Third Corps, was ordered by Meade to protect the southern side of Cemetery Ridge. Sickles's positioning of his troops toward the Emmitsburg Road gave the Confederates an opening in the Union line. Sickles exposed men could not be properly supported by the Union troops on his flanks.

If Lee's troops could have exploited the gap in the Union defense, Meade's forces would have been split and a Confederate victory at Gettysburg could have been a real possibility. Lee pushed his forces forward in an effort to achieve the victorious result he needed to fuel the Confederate hopes of winning the War between the States.

Late in the afternoon, two divisions of Confederate General Longstreet's Corps attacked the extensive line held by the Third Corps and the fighting raged from Devil's Den through the Wheatfield, to the Peach Orchard. At the height of the battle, General Sickles was disabled when a Confederate artillery shell smashed into his right leg. Beyond repair, the general's leg was amputated that evening.

Union troops were rushed to aid Sickles's Third Corps and Longstreet's assault on the Union left flank was thwarted.

* * *

As evening approached, the work of the Philadelphia Brigade was about to begin. The Confederates launched an attack on the Union army at about 6:30 p.m. The Confederates moved to the center of the Union defenses and the 69th Pennsylvania came under a direct assault. The 71st Pennsylvania was ordered by General Webb to support its fellow brigade unit. The two other regiments of the Philadelphia Brigade also joined in the fight at Webb's order of the "double-quick." The units quickly responded to Webb's order and engaged the enemy. Colonel Dewitt Baxter of the 72nd Pennsylvania was wounded in the exchange of fire.

General Webb lined up the 69th Pennsylvania and the unit poured fire into General Ambrose R. Wright's Rebel Brigade as soon as the Confederates topped the ridge, according to Embler's report. Wright's men began to run, and part of Webb's brigade chased them as far as the Emmitsburg Road, where they reclaimed a Union battery taken by the Rebels.

According to a history of the 71st Pennsylvania, members of the unit used a clump of trees in its front to give them some protection from the Rebels. The Southerners seized a brass cannon and turned the artillery piece belonging to Brown's Battery B, 1st Rhode Island Light Artillery on the Philadelphia Brigade. As the Rebels were loading the cannon, Colonel Richard Penn Smith ordered the 71st Pennsylvania to attack and were joined by elements of the 69th Pennsylvania.

The two units of the Philadelphia Brigade managed to drive off Wright's troops and recapture the brass cannon. The Union soldiers turned the weapon around and aimed the weapon on the retreating Southerners. Members of Webb's brigade were able to discharge the artillery piece as Rebel ranks scattered.

A report was written in 1889 by Anthony W. McDermott of the 69th Pennsylvania and delivered to the Ancient Order of Hibernians. The paper is contained at the Pennsylvania Historical Society and contains a segment about the engagement on the evening of July 2. "At 6:30 enemy assailed the position of the 69th as Wright's Georgia brigade made a furious assault, advancing obliquely from our left front. We met their charge with such a destroying fire that they were forced back in confusion. They rallied and made a second effort, lines broken and thinned as we pour volley upon volley into their disordered lines, until they finally retire a dispirited mob." The paper listed Captain M. Duffy of Company I and Lieutenant Charles Kelly as killed.

* * *

In a letter to Colonel John B. Bachelder on June 2, 1886, contained in the files of the Gettysburg National Military Park, McDermott wrote about the 69th Pennsylvania taking the field at Gettysburg. "We took no part in the fighting on the 1st of July, in fact we did not reach the vicinity of the battlefield until near midnight of the 1st, which we went into bivouac in a wood on the Taneytown road about one or two miles from Cemetery ridge the scene of our operations on the 2nd and 3rd of July.

"Shortly after daylight on the morning of the 2d, the regt. moved from the bivouac to Cemetery Ridge, and relieved the 90th Pennsylvania of the 1st Corps, our line of battle was formed immediately reaching the ridge, behind a stone wall about two feet high, and on the decline of the slope, facing the enemy and a short distance from the crest of the ridge, our right resting within about 15 or 20 paces of an angle of the wall that receded a short distance to the rear, left resting at an opening, or gateway through the wall. To the rear of the left of the right, was a cluster, or rather several small clusters of trees, these you have described to me as being the cluster not famous as the objective point in Pickett's advance upon our lines, while in the rear of right center, midway between our line of battle and the crest of the ridge was a small clump of trees with underbrush, these are what I was led to believe was the celebrated clump.

"Nothing occurred during the morning in our front, except some brisk picket firing until afternoon, when following the rout of the 3d Corps, which was driven past the prolongation of our line the enemy made a furious assault upon our line. To check his advance Brown's battery, dashed through the gateway upon our left, and stationed itself in front of our centre, and poured in a raking fire to the enemy's line; but still the enemy advanced charging upon the battery. Brown was forced to retire, leaving one piece behind. The enemy still advanced but before reaching this piece of artillery we opened a very destructive fire which compelled his line to halt. One of their officers succeeded in reaching the gun and sat upon the muzzle, urging his men to follow. He did not remain long in that position, our bullets removed him. Our men now dashed over the wall but General (William) Harrow who stood with our right, and (General Alexander) Webb, who was with our centre ordered us back to our position."[30]

McDermott wrote that he believed Pickett's Charge would not have taken place if the 69th were allowed to pursue the retreating Rebel troops on the evening of July 2. McDermott did say that Harrow and Webb must have had good reasons for ending the pursuit. McDermott described the death Captain Michael Duffy. "Duffy, who became angry at Gen. Harrow for not allowing us to charge the enemy, and when he saw the Rebel sitting on the piece of artillery, he became so exasperated that he stood upon the stone wall and directed us to oblique our fire and knock that d__d officer off the gun; scarcely had the words died away when he fell at the feet of Gen. Harrow, a ball having penetrated his head, a lifeless corpse. General Harrow expressed a great sorrow at losing so brave an officer."[31]

❉ ❉ ❉

Officers of the Philadelphia Brigade reported 40 casualties in the fight. When the area was secure, Webb's troops gathered a large number of rifles and other small arms left on the field. Colonel Richard Penn Smith of the 71st Pennsylvania was given credit for ordering the gathering of the weapons by one source. "Smith helped repulse the Confederates near Taneytown Road and then ordered men to gather weapons on the field and place them behind the stone wall."[32]

The weapons were placed to the rear of the stone wall being defended by the brigade. The gathered weapons would be put to good use by the Philadelphia Brigade the next day during Pickett's Charge.

The Confederate attack was driven off by the Union forces, including elements of the 106th and 72nd Pennsylvania. The Southerners retreated past the Emmitsburg Road towards Lee's main defense on Seminary Ridge. Reportedly, 250 Confederate prisoners were taken in the action, including 21 officers. The 72nd Pennsylvania reported capturing 20 prisoners.

General Webb's report of the late afternoon's engagement in the Official Records of the War of Rebellion stated, "The enemy made the assault of the 2d at about 6.30 p.m. Their line of battle advanced beyond one gun of Brown's battery, receiving at that point the fire of the Sixty-ninth Pennsylvania Volunteers and that of the Seventy-first Pennsylvania Volunteers, advanced to the support of the Sixty-ninth; also that of the One hundred and sixth and Seventy-second Pennsylvania Volunteers, which had previously been moved to the left, by command of Major-General Hancock.

"Colonel (DeWitt) Baxter, Seventy-second Pennsylvania Volunteers, at this time was wounded. They halted, wavered, and fell back, pursued by the One hundred and Sixth, Seventy-second, and part of the Seventy-first Pennsylvania Volunteers. The One hundred and sixth and Seventy-second Pennsylvania Volunteers followed them to the Emmitsburg road."[33]

After the engagement, the 106th Pennsylvania was ordered to join forces of General Oliver O. Howard of the 11th Army Corps near the civilian cemetery to the east of the position of the rest of the Philadelphia Brigade. The Rebels had pushed the Union forces back nearly to the Baltimore

Pike. Meade's defenses so far were holding on the crucial right flank of the Union army.

Soon after, Webb sent a second regiment, the 71st Pennsylvania, to answer a call for help on Culp's Hill. With Colonel Richard Penn Smith in command, the unit reported meeting Captain Craig Wadsworth and Captain Charles P. Horton, staff officers of General George Sears Greene. The staff officers ordered the unit to advance over rugged ground towards the area of Rock Creek. Smith authorized a cautious advance and detailed skirmishers to lead the way. Instead of meeting light resistance as Smith expected, the advance troops met a strong Rebel force and 19 members of the 71st Pennsylvania were captured. Another official report set the number of captured members of the unit as 14.

Colonel Smith's advance was stopped cold and his remaining troops were deployed along the Baltimore Pike to await an expected Confederate attack. No attack materialized and Smith returned his troops, without orders, to his original position on Cemetery Ridge along with the remaining elements of the Philadelphia Brigade. Smith was criticized for withdrawing his unit without orders but Smith contended the order given by the staff officers was unauthorized and he had no valid instructions to remain at Culp's Hill.

A more detailed description of Col. Smith's actions on Culp's Hill was given in the book *The History of Edward Baker's California Regiment*. "(Smith) was then ordered to support the 11th corps at Culp's Hill. They drifted to the right of their destination. 'I could find no general to report to who had command of any portion of the troops on the right,' Col. Smith wrote. He found Capt. Craig Wadsworth, a First Corps staff officer who conducted Smith and his men to the right of Brig. General George S. Greene's paper thin line. The right flank of the Army of the Potomac.

"Capt. Charles P. Horton, Green's assistant adjutant general, complained that the 71st 'was very slow in coming up.' Richard Penn Smith said he arrived 'on the ground under many disadvantages' and had no idea where Horton was leading his regiment. The staff officer assured the colonel 'that all was safe on either flank,' but Smith feared for the safety of his men.

"The 71st went into line, had about 20 skirmishers out and became engaged with the enemy on the front. They received fire from their right and rear. 'It was the heaviest and wickedest musketry fire for about half an hour that I ever laid under,' Sgt. (William) Burns wrote. But Horton had a different view and said the 71st were met by 'a few scattering shots from the front and from the right front' and little damage inflicted.

"Smith claimed he was being flanked. 'To my astonishment they retreated,' Horton wrote. Smith said he would not have the rest of his men murdered. Smith withdrew without orders even though at one point he said such order (existed).

"Smith took his men back to the original position and reported losses of three officers and 11 men captured. Second Lt. Byron C. Davis of Co. F was one of those captured and spent eight months in Libby Prison (Richmond, Virginia). (Sgt. William Burns) wrote that the Culp's Hill event 'as a blunder on the part of our officers (that) came near costing us dear.'"[34]

The action was described by Smith in a letter to General Isaac Jones Wistar on July 29, 1863. Smith reported that at about dark he was ordered to the support the 11th Corps and when he arrived he found the situation was different than he was told. Smith was told his flanks were protected. When Smith attacked the enemy to his front he received hostile fire from his right and to his rear. The Confederates had outflanked him. Smith believed his order to withdraw was correct. Smith wrote that his order was reviewed by superior officers without complaint. He reported losing three officers and 11 men taken as prisons of war.

A portion of General Hancock's report in the Official Records of the War of Rebellion concerning the Culp Hill fighting, stated, "It was nearly dark. Proceeding to the right of the Second Corps, near Cemetery Hill, and hearing a heavy engagement on General Howard's front, the firing seeming to come nearer and nearer, I directed General Gibbon to send Colonel Carroll's brigade, Third Division, to that point, to report to General Howard at once. I was gratified to hear subsequently, from General Howard in person, that it arrived at a very critical time, and that this unexpected re-enforcement materially assisted him in driving the enemy from his front.

"Hearing firing farther to the right, and believing it to be on General Slocum's front, and fearing that the troops he had sent to me had left him without sufficient force, I directed General Gibbon to send two regiments to that point. The Seventy-first Pennsylvania, Col. R. Penn Smith, and the One hundred and sixth Pennsylvania, Lieut. Col. W. L. Curry, were dispatched, but they also reported to Major-General Howard. The One hundred and sixth Pennsylvania Volunteers remained until relieved next day, doing good service. The Seventy-first returned to its command about midnight, without having received orders to do so, after suffering some loss."[35]

* * *

General John Gibbon, commanding the Second Division of the Second Corps, reported his observations of July 2 in the Official Records of the War of the Rebellion. The report was made from Baltimore, Maryland, a month after the battle of Gettysburg. Gibbon took over command of the Second Corps when General Hancock was ordered to take over direction of the center of the Union defenses including the Second and Third Corps.

Gibbon reported the placement of his troops on the morning of July 2 which was part of the famous "fish hook" defensive line utilized by General Meade at Gettysburg. Gibbon's right, the Third Division under General Alexander Hays, "rested near the cemetery and extended along the crest of a hill which, turning to the left, ran parallel to the turnpike and toward a prominent hill called Round Top. The Second Division came next, and the First Division (General John Caldwell) was upon the left, connecting with the third Corps.

"At the advance of the Third Corps at 4 p.m., the division

was in the following order: Webb's brigade on the right, partially behind a low stone wall, and protecting Cushing's battery, Fourth U.S. Artillery, which was on its right; Brown's Rhode Island battery was on Webb's left; Hall's brigade prolonged the line to the left, while Harrow's was held in reserve to the rear."[36]

Gibbon also described Sickles's ill-planned advance in his official report. "At 4 o'clock the Third Corps advanced, and, swinging round its left flank, took up a position along the Emmitsburg road. To give support to its right flank, I ordered forward two regiments of Harrows brigade, to occupy a position-along that road and to the right of a brick house. Here they tore down the fences and constructed breastworks, behind which they did most excellent service in checking the advance of the enemy, and preventing him from cutting off the Third Corps from our lines. For the same purpose, I sent a 12-pounder battery to the right and rear of these two regiments, to fire across the Emmitsburg road at some of the enemy's batteries established there.

"No sooner was the Third Corps in position, with its right resting near the brick house and the left 'in the air,' than the enemy made a most furious assault with infantry and artillery on that flank, rolling it back and enfilading the whole line. Such a flank attack could not be successfully resisted, and although dispositions were made to check the advance of the enemy, he came on so rapidly as to drive everything before him. I directed solid shot to be thrown from our batteries over the heads of our own men, and, on the application of General Humphreys, sent two of my regiments to his assistance.

"About this time the command of the (Second) corps was turned over to me by Major-General Hancock. The smoke was at this time so dense that but little could be seen of the battle, and I directed some of the guns to cease firing, fearing they might injure our own men or uselessly waste their ammunition.

"The Eighty-second New York and Fifteenth Massachusetts, near the brick house, were overpowered, outflanked by the enemy in pursuit of the Third Corps, and forced back after heavy loss, including both commanding officers. The Nineteenth Massachusetts, Colonel (Arthur) Devereux, and Forty-second New York, Colonel (James) Mallon, sent to the assistance of General Humphreys, finding themselves unable with that small force to stem the triumphant advance of the enemy, retired, after a short struggle, in good order.

"The enemy came on with such impetuosity that the head of his column came quite through a vacancy in our line to the left of my division, opened by detaching troops to other points. By the steadiness, however, of the troops in the immediate vicinity, and the timely arrival of the Twelfth Corps, this advance was checked and driven back with considerable loss, the pursuit being continued for some distance beyond our lines, and all the guns overrun by the enemy retaken. Darkness ended the contest here, but it continued for some time on our right, in front of the Eleventh

Corps. I sent Carroll's brigade, of the Third Division, and two regiments of Webb's brigade to its assistance."[37]

* * *

As the fighting subsided on the evening of July 2, 1863, along the front to be defended by the Philadelphia Brigade and other units of the Second Corps against Pickett's Charge, Union soldiers prepared for the next day's battle in different ways.

Lewis Rhell of Company F of the 72nd Pennsylvania recalled a conversation he had with his friend Captain John M. Steffan of Company A. Rhell wrote a letter on August 15, 1863, while at camp near Bealton Station, Virginia, describing that discussion.

"We had a small conversation (while resting) in which I asked him if he had any effects that I could keep for him till after the battle," the letter reported. "His reply was: 'Lew don't talk so foolish and make such big calculations. You don't think I am going to get killed do you?' Well John, I said, something tells me you are. (Just then the order was given to Forward.) 'Well Lew good bye,' off he went. I ran after him and asked if I could do anything if he should fall and his reply was 'Nothing Lew, Good bye.' I was with the rest of the drummers and fifers (we) were ordered to the hospital attending to the wounded men."[38]

Rhell's fear was realized as Steffan was wounded during the massive Southern cannonade preceding Pickett's Charge during the afternoon of July 3. The letter continued, "About one or two o'clock p.m. John was wounded. At that time the heavy shelling was going on. He (was) on the field about one hour when he was carried off the field by whom I do not know as I was at the V Corps Hospital at the time with the other musicians of our brigade. He was taken to the Stone hospital out near the field of battle or on the battlefield is more proper."

He recalled that about half past one or two in the afternoon an ambulance came into the hospital form the Stone house or, maybe the hospital, and he asked the driver if John was hurt. He said 'yes' and was at the stone house. Rhell immediately went to Doctor Aitkin and told him, The ambulance was sent back again for John's body, he recalled, but John couldn't be tumbled about as he was in so much pain, and there he laid, a large crowd of friends were around him. He was wounded and Rhell said he could only see him by looking through their legs. He saw two doctors at him dressing his wound. After 10 minutes when the storming rain of shells came and then Rhell and the doctors vacated the area and went behind a stone wall.

Rhell managed to reach the corps hospital again and stayed there until the Confederates were done shelling. He then saw John lying dead. Several were looking on when he came up, but soon went away. His pockets were turned inside out and I went into the house and inquired who had taken the things. The hospital steward said he had his watch and Doctor Aitken had all the other effects, which he was going to deliver to Col. Kockesberger. Rhell thought that was all right and did not ask for any of his things.

Chapter 4

PREPARATIONS

THE FIRST TWO days of hard fighting at Gettysburg were bloody and deadly, hectic and heroic and most of all, inconclusive. During the initial fighting, Confederate General Robert E. Lee's troops had come close several times to driving their Union foes from the field and forcing them closer to Washington, D.C. Every time the Rebels appeared to have won the battle the forces of Union General George Meade's Army of the Potomac found a way to stymie the Southern forces.

As generals in the camps of both armies pondered plans for July 3, 1863, the commanding officers were of the same mind on at least one thought another day of fighting had to take place at Gettysburg. Neither Lee nor Meade was in a position to break off the battle. Meade needed to defend Washington at all costs. A retreat would be considered a loss for Meade, the newly-minted commander of the Army of the Potomac in his first battle.

Lee was in a delicate position as the fighting concluded on July 2. His options were few. Retreating to Virginia was out of the question. A major victory on Union soil at Gettysburg would go a long way to winning independence for the South. A victory meant possible help from European nations. Another bloody defeat for the North, following the loss at Chancellorsville, could force the North to seek a negotiated end to the war. Indeed, Confederate President Jefferson Davis was making plans to seek such a negotiated peace. A Southern loss would preclude any help from foreign powers to the Southern cause and start an almost sure spiral to defeat.

Lee's options included holding and re-enforcing his strong defensive positions along Seminary Ridge and hoping that Meade would attack his forces—a sort of reverse Pickett's Charge. He could move his forces south and east towards Washington and force a battle at a different location. He could renew attacks on the flanks of Meade's army even though earlier attempts at Gettysburg failed to dislodge the Union forces. His other option was a frontal attack on the center of Meade's forces.

Holding a strong defensive line and having Meade order an advance would be the best outcome for Lee. The problem was Lee couldn't wait forever for Meade's attack because of limited supplies. Giving the North additional time could also mean additional troops being added to his enemy's columns, if additional troops were within marching distance of Gettysburg. Meade didn't have to accommodate Lee as Meade knew he could outwait the Southern commander.

Lee's generals, especially General James Longstreet, advocated a different location for a battle, one south of Gettysburg. Lee resisted the idea and one military scholar said if Lee followed Longstreet's advice, the move would result in the same frontal attack at a different hill with the same result. As for renewing the attacks on the Union flanks, Lee had no reason to believe additional fighting would gain a different result, especially since the Union army had reinforced its lines. Even so, Lee did not alter greatly his plans as July 3, 1863 began. The one viable option selected by Lee was a frontal attack on the center of Meade's line. The center of the line was thinly held by Union troops. Lee did not articulate his plans to his officers but his orders indicated a coordinated attack involving the taking of Culp's Hill, a charge on the Union rear by the cavalry of Jeb Stuart, a frontal attack by the fresh troops of General George Pickett on the Union center and a furious and destructive cannonading by the Southern artillery would give Lee and the South a much needed crucial victory.

Lee and Longstreet had mere hours to plan, coordinate and execute the most celebrated charge on American soil—Pickett's Charge.

* * *

General George Gordon Meade had major decisions facing him during the late night hours of July 2 and early morning hours of July 3. Should he attack, retreat or remain in place in his famous "fish hook" defensive position at Gettysburg? The placement of troops from the Round Tops through Cemetery Ridge and back to Culp's Hill resembled a fish hook.

Meade called a council of war and invited his top commanding officers to join him at his small headquarters at the farm of Lydia Leister. Leister, a widowed Pennsylvania Dutch woman, lived with her children in the small farmhouse when the outbreak of fighting took place at Gettysburg. One aide to Gibbon wrote, "When Meade arrived on the field he established his headquarters at a shabby little farmhouse on the left of the Taneytown Road, the house nearest the line and a little more than five hundred yards in rear of what became the centre of the position of the Second Corps."[39]

General John Gibbon described the setting of the meeting in a letter dated September 12, 1879. The person who received the letter is unknown but could have been an artist. The letter is in the files of the Gettysburg National Park at Gettysburg and states, "The Council at Gettysburg on the night of the 2nd of July 63 was held in one of the rooms of a small building which is still standing and which was occupied by Gnl. Meade as headquarter. The room was small and the centre of it occupied by a table at which sat Gen. Meade and Gen. Butterfield, his chief of staff.

"In the centre to the left as you enter the room from the kitchen stood a large four post bed on which during the session of the council, several of the members lounged. I think Gen. Sedgwick, Gen. Newton, and one or two others. The rest were distributed around the room, some of them sitting, others standing. In the corner at the foot of the bed, Gen. G. K. Warren, Chief of Eng. of the army, very tired, with a handkerchief tied round his neck to protect a wound he had received during the day laid sound asleep.

"It would be difficult to give you a position in relation to Gen. Hancock or any other member of the counsel. My dress was an old single-breasted blouse with Brg. Gen.

shoulder straps, pants stuffed with a long pair of muddy boots and a frayed cap, and I think most of the others were dressed in pretty much the same style. My complexion is light, my hair and beard a light brown, my eyes blue."[40]

General Gibbon was 36 years old at the time the Battle of Gettysburg was fought. He commanded the Second Corps and was wounded during Pickett's Charge, breaking his left shoulder. A West Point graduate, he was born in Philadelphia on April 20, 1827, the son of a physician. His family moved to North Carolina when he was 12 and his brothers fought for the South. He was described as "the most American of Americans, with his sharp nose and up-and-down manner of telling the truth, no matter whom it hurts."[41]

First Lieutenant Frank Aretas Haskell of the 6th Wisconsin Infantry served as an aide to Gibbon. Haskell described Gibbon at Gettysburg, writing, "He is compactly made, neither spare nor corpulent, with ruddy complexion, chestnut brown hair, with a clean-shaved face, except his moustache, which is decidedly reddish in color, medium-sized, well-shaped head, sharp, moderately jutting brows, deep-blue, calm eyes, sharp, slightly aquiline nose, compressed mouth, full jaws and chin, with an air of calm firmness in his manner. He always looks well dressed. (He is) fond of pipe smoking, an appreciation of good whiskey and an occasional use of bad words."[42]

Haskell described the meeting of the generals and reported present were George G. Meade, John Sedgwick, Henry W. Slocum, Oliver O. Howard, Winfield S.

Hancock, George Sykes, John Newton, Alfred Pleasanton and John Gibbon. He reported that Hancock was in charge of the 3rd Corps and Gibbon the 2nd Corps because of the wounding of General Dan Sickles on July 2. Also at the meeting were Generals Daniel Butterfield and Gouverneur K. Warren.

"Meade is a tall, spare man, with full beard, which with his hair, originally brown, is quite thickly sprinkled with gray, has a romanish face, very large nose, and a white large forehead, prominent and wide over the eyes, which are full and large, and quick in their movements, and he wears spectacles. His habitual personal appearance is quite careless, and it would be rather difficult (to) make him look well dressed. . . . Hancock is the tallest and most shapely, and in many respects is the best looking officer of them all. His hair is very light brown, straight and moist, and always looks well; his beard is of the same color, of which he wears the moustache and a tuft upon the chin; complexion ruddy, features neither large nor small, but well cut, with full jaw and chin, compressed mouth, straight nose full, deep blue eyes, and a very mobile, emotional countenance. He always dresses remarkably well, and his manner is dignified, gentlemanly, and commanding.

"They seemed fatigued, in the room was a large, wide bed in one corner, a small pine table in the centre upon which was a wooden pail of water, with a tin cup for drinking, and a candle and five or six straight-backed, rush-bottom chairs. The generals came in; some sat, some kept walking or standing, two lounged upon the bed, some were constantly smoking cigars. The questions discussed were to fall back to a stronger position, attack or wait an attack. They decided to wait for an attack. The meeting took about two hours."[43] Generally, all of the generals were in agreement to hold the field and readjust lines. Each corps commander gave an update on the condition of his unit before addressing the main issue of the night; if the Union army should attack and when, retreat or hold firm. According to an article in the *New York Times* of December 18, 1881, all of the generals favored waiting at least a day to see if Lee attacked. Some of the generals voiced other concerns. Under no circumstances, according to Gibbon, should Meade attack Lee. Newton and Hancock didn't want to press an attack or retreat but felt they shouldn't wait too long to force movement. Newton didn't want Lee to gain a stronger position. Hancock opined that if the North's communications were cut, an attack by Meade would be necessary. Howard offered that if the South hadn't attacked by 4:00 p.m. on July 3 that Meade should attack Lee. Slocum was adamant that the Army of the Potomac should stay and fight Lee's forces.

Newton had reservations about the defensive viability of the ground. Meade, according to the *New York Times* article, was quoted as saying, "Gettysburg was no place to fight a battle, but it was settled to remain."

The Official Records of the War of the Rebellion lists the minutes of council, July 3, 1863. According to participants, the minutes are not a full record of what was said. The original copy of the minutes were made in pencil and found among General Meade's papers. The Official Records of the War of the Rebellion minutes state:

> Questions asked:
> 1. Under existing circumstances, is it advisable for this army to remain in its present position or to retire to another nearer its base of supplies?
> 2. It being determined to remain in present position, shall the army attack or wait the attack of the enemy?
> 3. If we wait attack, how long?
>
> Replies:
>
> Gibbon:
> 1. Correct position of the army but would not retreat.
> 2. In no condition to attack, in his opinion.
> 3. Until he moves; until enemy moves.
>
> Williams:
> 1. Stay.
> 2. Wait attack.
> 3. One day.
>
> Birney:
> Same as General Williams.
>
> Sykes:
> Same as General Williams.
>
> Newton:
> 1. Correct position of the army, but would not retreat.
> 2. By all means not attack.

3. If we wait, it will give them a chance to cut our line.

Howard:
1. Remain.
2. Wait attack until 4 p.m. tomorrow.
3. If don't attack, attack them.

Hancock:
1. Rectify position without moving so as to give up field.
2. Not attack unless our communications are cut.
3. Can't wait long; can't be idle.

Sedgwick:
1. Remain, and wait attack at least one day.

Slocum:
Stay and fight it out.

Memorandum

Slocum:
Stay and fight it out.

Newton:
Thinks it is a bad position.

Hancock:
Puzzled about practicability of retiring; thinks by holding on (illegible word) to mass forces and attack.

Howard:
Favor of not retiring.

Birney:
Don't know; third Corps used up, and not in good condition to fight.

Sedwick:
Doubtful (remainder of sentence illegible.)
Effective strength (of Union army) 9,000, 12,500, 9,000, 6,000, 8,500, 6,000, 7,000; total, 58,000."[44]

The council disbursed and orders were drawn for the placement of troops and artillery for the upcoming battle. General Alexander Webb, commanding the focal point of the upcoming Confederate charge, made adjustments to his lines. At what was to become known as the Angle, two companies of the 71st Pennsylvania were placed just to the right of the 69th Pennsylvania. Less than 200 feet behind the two companies, six three-inch rifles of Lt. Alonzo H. Cushing's Battery A of the 4th United States Artillery stood ready for action. To the right of Cushing was Battery A, 1st Rhode Island commanded by Lt. William Arnold. After the cannonade, the remaining members of the 71st Pennsylvania were moved and completed the alignment at the Angle. In reserve behind Cushing's guns, was the 72nd Pennsylvania.

Webb ordered his units to fortify defenses but scant entrenching tools were available to help the troops. Fence rails had been dismantled and piled upon the stone wall. Colonel Norman J. Hall's Third Brigade, destined to play an important part in the repulse of Pickett's Charge, did what it could to bolster protection. "During the night the line was strengthened as much as possible with rails, stones, and earth thrown up with sticks and boards, no tools being obtainable," Hall's report stated. Hall's troops included the 7th Michigan, 42nd and 59th New York and 19th and 20th Massachusetts plus some Massachusetts sharpshooters. Members of Webb's Philadelphia Brigade did search the grounds where the recent fighting took place to secure abandoned weapons and ammunition. Hundreds of rifles were gathered. Some men awaited Pickett with a dozen loaded weapons at their side.

Gibbon wrote in his *Personal Recollections of the Civil War*, "It was near on to midnight when the council broke up and then Hancock, Newton and I repaired to a yard near the next house (to) Meade's Headquarters (Brown's) and all three crawling into my Headquarters ambulance, slept till waked up early the next morning by heavy picket firing on our left near Round Top. Everybody was soon astir, but the morning wore away and nothing very remarkable seemed to be taking place although every now and then the cannon on either side would open or a sudden spurt of picket firing would take place showing that both sides were alert and ready for slaughter—when the chiefs gave the word."

Gibbon couldn't recall how he spent morning but he remembered servants at one point made coffee and lunch. An old and tough rooster was prepared for the pot and made into a stew, Gibbon recalled. The general went to Meade's headquarters and found the commanding general looking worn and haggard. Meade said he hadn't eaten since breakfast. Meade at first rejected Gibbon's offer to join him for lunch, saying he had to remain at his headquarters to receive reports which were constantly coming to him. Gibbon pointed out that they would be close and he would be absent but a few minutes. Gibbon urged Meade to keep up his physical strength. Meade relented and shared with Gibbon coffee and stewed rooster.

Lieutenant Haskell recalled that General Gibbon woke him at 4:00 a.m. by pulling on his feet. Gunfire greeted Haskell as sharp skirmishing was taking place.[45] Haskell also wrote the sun shone during the morning, a rarity in recent days. Haskell also overheard some wishful thinking among his comrades as some soldiers, while making coffee and preparing hardtack, said they believed Lee wouldn't give battle that day.

Haskell was more practical than his fellow soldiers. "I could not help wishing all the morning that this line of the divisions of the Second Corps were stronger; it was, so far as numbers constitute strength, the weakest part of our whole line of battle."[46] Confederate General Lee was thinking along the same lines as Haskell.

Haskell also added some details to the lunch featuring the tough rooster. "(We had) lunch of a few chickens, bread, butter and John the cook (prepared) stewed chicken, potatoes and toast. Some of the generals gathered and a few lit cigars to talk of yesterday's battle. Hancock took control of Second Corps and Gibbon the Second Division. Gibbon asked Capt. Farrell of 1st Minnesota, who commanded the Provost Guard of his division, to join him. I never saw him again. He was killed, in two or three hours."[47]

Hancock's report in the Official Records of the War of the Rebellion detailed some of the preparations taking place before daybreak on July 3, including the crucial replenishing of artillery shells. "During the night of the 2d, the batteries were supplied with ammunition as far as practicable. Having brought but half the ammunition train of the corps, we were dependent somewhat on others. The battery ammunition was supplied by the train of the Artillery Reserve, though not to the full extent required.

"The corps had been so weakened by its losses on the 2d, that on the 3d instant it required every available man in the line of battle to cover the ground held the previous day. Colonel Carroll's brigade, of General Hays' division, was retained by General Howard, and, with the exception of the Eighth Ohio, was not engaged with the Second Corps during the day.

"The early morning passed in comparative quiet along our front, but the heavy and continued firing on the right indicated that the efforts of the enemy were being directed on the Twelfth Corps. Trifling affairs occurred at intervals between the enemy's skirmishers and our own, and the artillery of the corps was frequently and successfully engaged with that of the enemy."[48]

Sergeant Frederick Fuger's morning wasn't quiet. Fuger, a member of Cushing's Battery A of the 4th United States Field Artillery at Gettysburg, wrote about his experiences and his renderings are part of the records of the Gettysburg National Military Park. He wrote, "July 3 in the morning about 8 a.m. enemy opened fire and exploded three limber of Battery A. Gen. Hunt. Lt. Cushing and myself were standing behind No. 3 limber when explosion took place.

"To our surprise not a single man or horse was injured.

Horses ran away but were stopped by some of our infantry. When the Confederates saw this explosion they immediately jumped up and gave an immense yell. We replied and within five minutes an explosion took place in their line . . . our men jumped up and returned the compliment. The firing lasted about 30 minutes. Up to 11 a.m. we engaged the enemy's artillery four times, each lasting about 10 minutes. From 11 a.m. until 1 p.m. there was a perfect lull."[49]

Fuger survived Gettysburg and Pickett's Charge and attained the rank of lieutenant colonel during the Civil War. A native of Goppingen, Württemberg, (modern day Germany) he fought in 63 battles and died on October 13, 1913, and is buried in Arlington Cemetery, Washington, D.C.

Troops in both armies were enduring a hot and humid July 3. One report indicated the day dawned sultry and became oppressively hot as the sun burned through the haze about noon. The diary of Joseph P. Elliot, Quartermaster of the 71st Pennsylvania, included a weather report that stated early morning clouds with winds from the southwest. The skies cleared about noon but the weather was hot. Elliot added that he could hear heavy firing in the direction of Gettysburg.

The companies of the 106th Pennsylvania were split as July 3 began. The majority of the regiment was on Cemetery Hill under the command of Lieutenant Colonel William L. Curry. Captain Robert Ford stood with 50 men on picket duty in front of the rest of the Philadelphia Brigade troops. Companies A and B were positioned in reserve behind the crest of the hill. About 40 percent of the 106th Pennsylvania would be involved in the repulse of Pickett's Charge.

General Gibbon took time to pen a letter to his wife at 10:30 a.m. on the hot and humid morning, just hours before Pickett's Charge. The letter states, "Today there has been more or less artillery and picket firing going on but no general fight and both armies are tired enough to remain quiet for some hours longer.

"We can afford to wait better than the rebels, and I hope before many hours are over Lee's Army will be so disabled as to render any further harm in this part of the country impossible. God has been very good to me dear Mama (wife) in protecting me from so many dangers. Poor Reynolds and Weed were both killed the battle yesterday. Kiss the dear children for me, write often.

"Yours J.G."[50]

Gibbon's hope would be fulfilled as Lee's army would be defeated but not before many soldiers of the Army of the Potomac would die in the assault known as Pickett's Charge.

Chapter 5

MOST INFERNAL PANDEMONIUM

Major Samuel Roberts of the 72nd Pennsylvania was standing in the heat on open ground near the copse of trees that soon would be the deadly goal of more than 10,000 advancing Southern troops. Roberts was listening to one of his sergeants talk "about some girls in Philadelphia"[51]

The talk of home and civilian topics abruptly ceased as the first shell fired by Robert E. Lee's Washington Artillery of New Orleans whistled towards the Philadelphia Brigade. "All hell broke out," Roberts remembered.[52] Colonel Richard Penn Smith added, "My God, it was terrible. . . . Such a sight you never saw. The air appeared to be thick with cannon balls. The destruction caused by them was the most severe I had ever seen."[53]

Sergeant Ben Hirst of 14th Connecticut wrote his wife, "Turn your eyes which way you will the whole Heavens were filled with Shot and Shell, Fire and Smoke."[54]

Lee had unleashed approximately 140 artillery pieces on the Union troops holding the middle of General George G. Meade's line. The shells that would fly from Seminary Ridge for more than an hour would cause damage to the Union forces, as Smith reported, but the shelling didn't inflict a crippling blow to the Union troops as Lee expected.

The accuracy of that initial round from Lee's Washington

Artillery is in question. Author Carol Reardon wrote in her *Pickett's Charge in History and Memory*, "But from the moment the Washington Artillery fired the first signal shot to open the cannonade, the historical record clouds considerably. Indeed, accounts of the fate of that first shot, as eyewitnesses record it, provide a foretaste of the fog of war that invests all that follows. Depending on whom one chooses to believe, that projectile nearly cut in two Lt. S. S. Robinson of the 19th Massachusetts; or it sailed harmlessly over an officer of that same regiment who lay wounded in a hospital way behind the front lines; or it exploded behind the Vermont brigade; or it was a dud that hit near the lines of the 12th New Jersey; or it exploded on a rock in the 12th New Jersey's line, scattering gravel all over nearby soldiers."[55]

Philadelphia born Colonel James G. Biddle, a grandson of an American Revolution officer, also reported hours of perfect quiet took place before the Southern artillery opened. "Our batteries, posted by General (Henry) Hunt, the efficient Chief of Artillery, replied with about 70 guns. This artillery duel, which lasted about an hour and a half, was the most severe experienced anywhere during the war. The air was filled with bursting shell and solid shot and the very earth shook with the resounding cannon."[56] Biddle served with several units during the Civil War, including the 6th Indiana Cavalry.

Biddle wrote that the Philadelphia Brigade was rallied by the personal efforts of its commander, General Alexander Webb. According to eyewitness reports, during the Confederate artillery barrage Webb made sure the members of his new command saw him. One report had Webb standing in front of the line, leaning on his sword and puffing on a cigar. He is said to have ignored shouts of his men to take cover. One solider later wrote that Webb stood like a statue as he observed movements of the enemy. Webb later recalled that he felt like all of the Confederate artillery pieces were training their sites on him. "This was awful," he wrote. Webb recalled that he was struck three or four time with stones and other debris from the spent shells.

There was no doubt in Webb's mind that his Philadelphia Brigade was about to receive a fierce infantry attack and the bombardment was just a prelude to the main assault.

Lieutenant Anthony McDermott of the 69th Pennsylvania described the bombardment in a letter to Colonel John B. Bachelder in a letter written on June 2, 1886, and contained in the Bachelder files at Gettysburg National Military Park. "The morning of the 3d passed off quietly except for the usual picket firing, sometimes very brisk and again all quiet until about noon. The troops had all finished eating their stew, or sipping their coffee, when a death-like stillness prevailed throughout the army. The sun was shining in all its glory giving forth a heat almost stifling and not a breath of air came to cause the slightest quiver to the most delicate leaf, or blade of grass.

"The sound of a Whitworth gun was the first to break that stillness, it came from the Rebel lines and its shots passed high over our heads, a minute or two elapsed then there was opened a volley of artillery, shot and shell, that ploughed through the air, ground and over our heads."[57]

Lieutenant Frank Haskell, General John Gibbon's aide, wrote about glancing at his watch and noting the time was 12:55 p.m. Haskell had thought it would be a good time to take a nap. He was wrong. "The report of gun after gun, in rapid succession, smote our ears, and their shells plunged down and exploded all around us. We sprang to our feet. In briefest time the whole Rebel line to the west was pouring out its thunder and its iron upon our devoted crest. The wildest confusion for a few moments obtained among us. The shells came bursting all about."[58]

Haskell witnessed first hand the terror caused by the shelling, including the maiming and killing of soldiers and the explosion of two of Lieutenant Alonzo Cushing's limber boxes. "We could not often see the shell before it burst, but sometimes, as we faced towards the enemy, and looked above our heads, the approach would be heralded by a prolonged hiss, which always seemed to me to be a line of something tangible, terminating in a black globe, distinct to the eye, as the sound had been to the ear. The shell would seem to stop, and hang suspended in the air an instant, and then vanish in fire and smoke and noise. We saw the missiles tear and plow the ground. All in rear of the crest for a thousand yards, as well as among the batteries, was the field of their blind fury."[59] While most of the shells overshot the Union infantry, damage was done to support troops on the other side of the slope.

Sergeant Frederick Fuger, serving with Cushing, wrote, "It was the most terrific cannonade I ever witnessed. The whole Confederate line was in a blaze of fire. The very earth shook beneath our feet. The splash of bursting shells and shrapnel and the fierce neighing of wounded artillery horses, made a picture terrible grand and sublime."[60] In almost no time, a traffic jam took place on Taneytown Road as ambulances with wounded men were clogging the route to field hospitals. Haskell described Meade's headquarters being struck several times. Horses of officers and orderlies were lying dead around the small farmhouse of widow Lydia Leister. "Rider less horses galloped madly through the fields."[61]

General Meade wrote about the status of his Gettysburg headquarters at the time of the shelling in a letter to Colonel John Badger Bachelder on December 4, 1869. Meade said it was suggested his headquarters be moved to safer ground but he wanted to be where officers could find him. Meade wrote, "The house was situated about 300 or 400 yards in the rear of the line of battle and about the centre of the enemy's converging lines of fire."[62] Meade wrote he later ordered headquarters moved to a hill on Baltimore Pike where General Henry Slocum had his headquarters. Meade found the new location to be as exposed to fire as the Leister farm. Meade wrote he returned to the old headquarters. Separated from his staff and on way back Meade found several officers, including his son. Lieutenant George Meade of the 6th Pennsylvania Cavalry had his horse killed during the action.

"On the Taneytown Road a marching column of Henry Eustis's brigade of the Sixth Corps, returning from the duty at Culp's Hill, was caught in the rain of shells. 'Solid shot would strike the large rocks and split them as if exploded by gunpowder,' wrote diarist Elisha Hunt Rhodes. 'The flying iron and pieces of stone struck men down in every direction,'" wrote author Stephen W. Sears in his book *Gettysburg*. Sears also reported shells hit the foundation and front porch of Meade's headquarters, about 400 yards beyond the center of his line. Sixteen horses died at the farmhouse and Meade's Chief of Staff, General Alexander Butterfield, was wounded as Meade's headquarter was relocated to a safer position. "The plain behind the ridge was almost immediately swept of all camp followers and the unordered attendants of an army," Sears quoted the Second Corps's historian as writing. The description came from a report by General Winfield Scott Hancock.

General Gibbon's report filed with the Official Records of the War of the Rebellion was brief concerning the artillery barrage. He reported skirmishing took place at times all along the line during the morning and some little artillery firing occurred. Gibbon reported at 1:00 p.m. the enemy opened with artillery all along his line. He wrote that for two hours the most terrific shower of shot and shell took place. He also noted the Union batteries ably responded to the Confederate fire. At the time, Gibbon said he returned to his division as General Hancock resumed command of the corps.

Gibbon, a former artillery officer, had more to say about the artillery barrage in his personal remembrances. He wrote about the higher velocity rifled shells coming screaming at his troops. When the shell started to tumble through the air, troopers had the impression that they were liable to be hit no matter where they stood. Indeed, one of the first shells killed Gibbon's orderly. Gibbon also couldn't locate his horse. The scene, Gibbon wrote, was "the most infernal pandemonium it has ever been my fortune to look upon." When the first shot was fired Gibbon and the rest of the officers rushed to their commands. The files of the Gettysburg National Military Park contain Gibbon's *Personal Recollections of the Civil War*. The following is his account.

A single round was heard off in my front and everyone's attention was attracted. Almost instantly afterwards the whole air above and around us was filled with bursting and screaming projectiles, and the continuous thunder of the guns, telling us that something serious was at hand. All jumped to their feet and loud calls were made for horses. Mine did not come up at once and anxious to get upon my line, I started on a run, up a little swale leading directly up to the center of it. The features of that hurried trip are indelibly impressed upon my memory. The thunder of the guns was incessant, for all of ours had now opened fire and the whole air seemed filled with rushing, screaming and bursting shells. The larger round shells could be seen plainly as in their nearly completed course they curved in their fall towards the Taneytown road, but the long rifled shells came with a rush and a scream and could only be seen in their rapid flight when they 'upset' and went tumbling through the air, crating the uncomfortable impression that, no matter whether you were in front of the gun from which they came or not, you were liable to be hit.

Every moment, or so one would burst, throwing its fragments about or first striking the ground plough a furrow in the earth and rocks, throwing theses last about in a way as dangerous as the pieces of the exploding shell. At least I reached the brow of the hill to find myself in the most infernal pandemonium it has ever been my fortune to look upon. Very few troops were in sight and those that were, were hugging the ground closely, some behind the stone wall, some not, but the artillerymen were all busily at work at their guns, thundering out defiance to the enemy whose shells were bursting in and around them at a fearful rate, striking now a horse, now a limber box, and now a man. Looking thus at Cushing's Battery, my eyes happened to rest upon one of the gunners standing in rear of the nearest limber, the lid open showing the charges. Suddenly, with a shriek, came a shell right under the limber box, and the poor gunner went hopping to the rear on one leg, the shreds of the other dangling about as he went.

As I reached the line just to the left of Cushing's battery, I found Gen. Webb seated on the ground as coolly as though he had not interest in the scene.... Of course, it would be absurd to say we were not scared. 'What does this mean?' I asked. Webb shook this head. It might mean preparation for retreat; it might signify the prelude to an assault.

A position farther to the front would be safer and rising to my feet, I worked forward accompanied by my aide (Lt. Haskell). I made but a few steps when three of Cushing's limber boxes blew up at once, sending the contents in a vast column of dense smoke high in the air. (At the copse of tress and wall) nothing could be seen except the smoke from the long line of batteries and nothing heard but the continuous roar of hundreds of guns. These (Confederate shells) all went over our heads and generally burst behind us.[63]

* * *

Long before Lee's artillery opened on the center of Meade's line, units of the Philadelphia Brigade were engaged with elements of Lee's army. Throughout the morning of July 3, 1863, skirmishing took place, especially around the farm of William Bliss. The farm was centrally located between the opposing armies. A sturdy farmhouse and outbuildings provided cover for Confederate sharpshooters. Artillery on both sides joined in the fray and one Confederate shot struck a limber under Cushing's command. The explosion rocked the nearby Rhode Island unit and scattered the horses attached to Cushing's artillery unit.

In front of the Union batteries were the men of the 69th Pennsylvania. They had to endure the shelling from the Southern artillery units and also the concussion waves set off by their own artillery. The ear-drum splitting noise and the noxious black smoke made life uncomfortable for the units of the Philadelphia Brigade. "After the cannonading began, we were all hugging the earth and we would have liked to get into it if we could," Joseph McKeever of Company E, 69th Pennsylvania recalled.[64]

"Christopher Smith of Cushing's battery wrote that 'the smoke became so dense that we could see nothing on the other side of the valley. It was a bright day, but the sun through the smoke looked like a great red ball . . . all around was a great cloud of smoke.' General Gibbon recalled that 'over all hung a heavy pall of smoke underneath which could be seen the rapidly moving legs of the men as they rushed to and from between the pieces and line of limbers, carrying forward the ammunition.'"[65]

Some of the Confederate artillery shells found their mark and exploded within the units of the Federal artillery causing disfiguring injuries and horrific deaths. Heads ands limbs were sheared from bodies of soldiers. As casualties mounted within the artillery ranks, some members of the Philadelphia Brigade rushed to aid the undermanned artillery pieces. The members of the brigade and the rest of the troops stood firm despite the deadly shells. Indeed, John Harvey Jr. of Company A of the 69th Pennsylvania was reported to have lost his life during the shelling.

As the Confederate batteries targeted Cushing's guns, the officers of the Philadelphia Brigade ordered their men to lie prone as to protect them somewhat from the pounding of the Southern guns. Colonel Dennis O'Kane of the 69th Pennsylvania noted the order wasn't needed as his men had already flattened themselves on the ground. O'Kane, positioned near the copse of trees, had an excellent view as the Union batteries kept returning fire despite severe losses of men and artillery pieces.

Captain Frank Haskell of Gibbon's staff also noted the posting of the men of the brigade. About 2:00 p.m. Haskell wrote he was among the infantry. Haskell and the Philadelphia Brigade members reported they were thankful that the Confederate artillery officers couldn't find the range and overshot their position. The men even had time to make jokes about the inaccuracy of the Southern gunners.

"They lay there flat upon the earth a little to the front of the batteries," Haskell wrote. "They were suffering little and were quiet and cool. How glad we were that the enemy was no better gunners, and that they cut the shell fuses too long. . . . And so they lay under the heaviest cannonade that ever shook the continent, and among them a thousand times more jokes than heads were cracked."[66]

As the artillery dual reached its zenith, General Winfield Scott Hancock patrolled the ground his troops were to defend in the coming hours. Hancock was earning his nickname of "Hancock the Superb" as he was making every effort to place his men in the best position to repulse the Confederate assault he expected to take place. The sheer force of his presence dominated the defense at the Angle, fellow Union officers noted. Hancock's nickname among the Southern army, according to Confederate General John B. Gordon, was "Thunderbolt of the Army of the Potomac."

A soldier who witnessed Hancock that day stated "his daring and heroism and splendid presence gave the men new courage."[67]

Hancock's opponents that hot day of July 3, 1863, weren't limited to the Confederates. He became involved in a heated argument with the Army of the Potomac's chief of artillery, General Henry Jackson Hunt.

* * *

General Hunt, a veteran of the Mexican War where he was twice wounded, fought well in many of the Civil War battles before Gettysburg. Late in the morning of July 3, 1863, Hunt rode to the crest of Cemetery Ridge and made an observation about his opponent's artillery. "Here a magnificent display greeted my eyes. Our whole front for two miles was covered by batteries already in line or going into position. They stretched . . . from opposite the town to the Peach Orchard, which bounded the view to the left, the ridges of which were thick with cannon. Never before had such a sight been witnessed on this continent. What did it mean?"[68]

What Hunt was observing was Confederate Colonel Edward P. Alexander lining up as many as 150 cannons in an attempt to wreck the Union defenses on Cemetery Ridge. When the Confederates opened the cannonade, "Surprised Union artillerymen ran to their cannon and returned fire. The battlefield shook under the weight of explosions. Fire and dense smoke covered the ridges and rolled across the fields. Gunners toiled over their heated guns as shells churned up the earth around them, knocking men and horses to the ground. Caissons and limber chests of two Union batteries erupted in massive explosions."[69]

Hunt spent part of his morning moving Union artillery into position to meet the Confederate threat. The artillery reserve section was stationed nearby to provide relief when needed. When batteries near the center of the Union line ran low on ammunition or were destroyed by Confederate shelling, Hunt ordered replacements from the reserves. Some batteries attempted to leave the front line but didn't have enough horses to pull out the artillery pieces as many of the animals were killed or maimed during the barrage.

The reply shelling of the Union artillery bolstered the spirits of the Philadelphia Brigade and the other Union troops in the line of Confederate fire. The dispute between generals Hunt and Hancock came about when Hunt stopped firing to conserve ammunition for the expected infantry charge. Hancock didn't want the Union artillery to cease firing. He believed keeping the morale of his troops high was worth the use of the precious ammunition. The dispute became very personal after the war as the two generals traded accusations about Hunt's order to conserve ammunition.

Tactically, Hunt may have been correct in trying to preserve resources but the psychological affect on Hancock's men could have been devastating if the shelling reduced the men's will to fight. As Colonel Francis Walker of Hancock's staff wrote, "Every soldier knows how trying and demoralizing it is to endure artillery fire without reply," The artillery batteries in the open near the Philadelphia Brigade also were thankful for the firing of their fellow units."

General Hancock braved the fire of the Confederates

by inspecting his lines while on horseback with an orderly displaying the Second Corps flag. Staff officers warned Hancock not to put his life in jeopardy by so boldly presenting himself to the enemy. Hancock replied, "There are times when a corps commander's life does not count."[70]

Hancock was known for his temper and the cessation of firing of the Union artillery triggered an outburst. Captain John Hazard, Hancock's chief of artillery for the Second Corps, informed Hancock of Hunt's order to save the shells for the expected infantry attack. Hancock informed Hazard that he, Hancock, was in charge and he should resume firing his guns. Hancock next turned to the battery of the 15th New York, commanded by Captain Patrick Hart. Hancock's inflamed orders were the same to Hart as they were to Hazard. Hart described the tone of his commander's order as "profane and blasphemous such as a drunken ruffian would use."[71]

Hancock's overbearing manner didn't intimidate one officer, Colonel Freeman McGilvery. McGilvery stood by the orders of General Hunt.

Hunt and every other Union officer believed a Confederate charge was imminent. They also believed the sooner Lee's troops attacked, the better chance Union troops would have to successfully defend the Union center. A cessation of Union artillery fire might encourage Lee's troops to begin the attack. Also, Hunt received word from Union officers on Little Round Top that the Union shelling was ineffective. General Gouverneur K. Warren, known as the savior of Little Round Top for his quick action in defending the pivotal position at Gettysburg on July 2, reported to General George G. Meade that the Union shelling was only filling the valley with smoke.

Hunt sent a message to General Meade informing him of his decision to stop returning Confederate fire. In a letter Hunt authored on January 6, 1866, he explained that early during the day of July 3, 1863, he believed Lee would mount a grand assault on the middle of the Union line. Hunt said he ordered his battery commanders to "not return the fire for fifteen or twenty minutes at least, that they must watch closely the effect of the enemy's cannonade; not the most efficient part of his lines, which they would probably find to be the one on which most guns were placed, and to concentrate our fire on that point, firing slowly, deliberately and making target practice of it.

"The motives of this order were threefold, first, we occupied the chord of the arc on which the enemy assembled his batteries, and therefore could bring fewer guns into action than he could and a part of our chord was so broken by woods and rock, that only a portion of it could be used, thus further diminishing our number of effective guns. Second, we must make up for this by the superior effect of our fire, from close observations, deliberate, slow and sure practice, aiming low; and third, as the cannonade of the enemy was to proceed and assault, it was of vital importance that when his fire ceased, we should have in the chests a sufficient reserve of ammunition to sustain a rapid and effective fire from all our batteries on the advancing infantry from the moment it emerged from the woods.

"I ordered the cessation of our fire, gradually from right to left to induce the enemy to believe he had silenced us, and to precipitate his assault. Didn't have time to examine all of the batteries and didn't those in Second Corps. I learned that General Hancock, as soon as the enemy opened fire, ordered all his own (2nd Corps) and other batteries near him to open in reply, that on my orders being repeated to him, he said his troops would not stand unless the reply was made, and that he would be responsible to me for the disregard of my instructions. The batteries attached to his corps obeyed his orders; those of the Artillery Reserve under Col. McGilvery refused to do so. These latter were accordingly fully prepared for the assault which followed." [72]

In another letter dated February 1882 contained in the Bachelder Papers at the National Park Service, Gettysburg, Hunt responded to a charge by General Hancock that Hunt had obstructed the defense at the Angle when he ordered guns to stop firing on the enemy. Hunt quoted Hancock as saying, "I was actually compelled to threaten force, on my own line of battle before I could cause the battery to fire upon the enemy." Hunt stated Hancock's artillery "had thrown away in an utterly useless cannonade every round of its long range ammunition, and therefore it could not open on the advancing troops until they came within canister range of his 12 pounder batteries. Of course the fire was 'feeble' for the rifle batteries were still ineffective, their canister range being less than half that of the 12 pounders. He (Hancock) complains that I had ordered all the artillery both of the Second Corps and of the reserve, to withhold its fire. That is true, and it was with the object of making the advancing troops pass through, not a 'feeble fire of artillery' but a heavy cross-fire from the whole line from the first moment of their advance and before they came under infantry fire. His counter orders, to 'secure obedience' to which he was as he himself says 'actually compelled to threaten force' resulted in the artillery fiasco he describes and moreover in a fearful loss of like and a narrow escape from defeat."[73]

Hunt wrote to Colonel John Bachelder that he regretted "the necessity of entering upon matters of a more personal nature, although connection with the same subjects, but some of Major General Hancock's statements are such as would brand me with disgrace if not met and refuted."[74]

The same Bachelder Papers contain a letter from Captain Andrew Cowan of the 1st New York Independent Battery, Artillery Brigade of the Sixth Corps. Cowan wrote, "I was ordered soon after daylight, July 3rd, to report to Gen. Newton (commanding the 1st corps) with my battery. Arrived at the piece of woods in which he had his headquarters. And found he was out on the line. I reported to General (Abner) Doubleday. We went to the front and decided not to put my guns there in fear of drawing enemy fire. Moved back 100 yards and parked. Moved forward after Rebels began the cannonading. During the hottest of the fire, an aide galloped through my battery and cried to me 'to reserve all my fire for the infantry.' Then ordered to see Gen. (Alexander) Webb but under Doubleday orders. Saw an officer with hat waving from higher ground and believed needed to move at risk of disobeying orders moved gun to the spot. Webb pointed to the front and I then knew what reserving my fire for the infantry meant. Before too smoky to see. We opened at once and continued pouring fire. And then to canister when within range. Then came the severe struggle. Our infantry which was a half dozen yards in front of my guns, lying down, all at once became panic stricken and broke in confusion."[75]

* * *

General Hancock did give credit to the artillery units attached to Second Corps as he described his actions before Pickett's Charge on July 3 in his report recorded in the Official Records of the War of the Rebellion.

The early morning passed in comparative quiet along our front, but the heavy and continued firing on the right indicated that the efforts of the enemy were being directed on the Twelfth Corps. Trifling affairs occurred at intervals between the enemy's skirmishers and our own, and the artillery of the corps was frequently and successfully engaged with that of the enemy.

From 11 a.m. until 1 p.m. there was an ominous stillness. About 1 o'clock, apparently by a given signal, the enemy opened upon our front with the heaviest artillery fire I have ever known. Their guns were in position at an average distance of about 1,400 yards from my line, and ran in a semicircle from the town of Gettysburg to a point opposite Round Top Mountain. Their number is variously estimated at from one hundred and fifteen to one hundred and fifty. The air was filled with projectiles, there being scarcely an instant but that several were seen bursting at once. No irregularity of ground afforded much protection, and the plain in rear of the line of battle was soon swept of everything movable. The infantry troops maintained their position with great steadiness, covering themselves as best they might by the temporary but trifling defenses they had erected and the accidents of the ground. Scarcely a straggler was seen, but all waited the cessation of the fierce cannonade, knowing well what it foreshadowed. The artillery of the corps, imperfectly supplied with ammunition, replied to the enemy most gallantly, maintaining the unequal contest in a manner that reflected the highest honor on this arm of the service. Brown's battery (B, First Rhode Island), which had suffered severely on the 2d, and expended all of its canister on that day, retired before the cannonading ceased, not being effective for further service. The remaining batteries continued their fire until only canister remained to them, and then ceased.

After an hour and forty-five minutes, the fire of the enemy became less furious, and immediately their infantry was seen in the woods beyond the Emmitsburg road, preparing for the assault.[76]

* * *

While the debate continued about the wisdom of returning the Confederate fire, Southern shells were damaging the batteries of the Second Corps, especially those positioned among the men of the Philadelphia Brigade. Captain James Rorty, commanding Battery B, 1st New York, had two artillery pieces knocked out of action and many men disabled. Members of the 19th Massachusetts were detailed to help keep the remaining two guns of Rorty's battery functioning.

Battery B, 1st Rhode Island was withdrawn under heavy fire after one of its cannons was struck just as it was being loaded and ammunition was running low. Battery A of the same Rhode Island unit later followed to the rear of Cemetery Ridge after running out of shells during the Confederate infantry charge.

Standing tall and returning fire during the bombardment was Lieutenant Alonzo Cushing's Battery A of the 4th United States Artillery. An 1861 West Point graduate, Cushing worked his guns as the enemy shells were taking a toll on his unit. So many of his own men were wounded and killed that infantry members had to be pressed into service for his guns. Those infantry soldiers also became casualties, one even shooting himself to death after receiving a grievous wound.

Cushing didn't escape the shelling of the Confederates as he suffered two painful wounds, one to his shoulder and the other to his groin. Despite the urging of his men to go to the rear and receive treatment, Cushing remained at his station. "I stay right here and fight it out or die in the attempt," Cushing said.[77]

Around Cushing General Webb's Philadelphia Brigade was also losing valuable men. The brigade defending the center of the Union line was undermanned from the start and the casualties made the thin defensive line thinner. Webb wrote to his wife that that he had lost 50 of his men and officers from the Confederate artillery bombardment. Some of the men from the 71st Pennsylvania commanded by Colonel Richard Penn Smith were ordered to help Cushing's battery. The bombardment "made frightful decimation in the ranks of the Philadelphia Brigade" Smith wrote.[78] Smith noted that some of the casualties included Private J. Kavanaugh of Company B, a 21-year-old soldier who was wounded in his left thigh and suffered a compound fracture of his skull from a piece of a shell, and Captain John Steffan who was wounded in the chest.

Adjutant Anthony W. McDermott of the 69th Pennsylvania vividly wrote in 1889 about the effects of the Confederate artillery fire on the Philadelphia Brigade. "The air is filling with the whirring, shrieking, hissing sounds of solid shot and the bursting of shell; all throw themselves flat upon the ground, behind the low stone wall. (Shells) went sometimes in volleys, again in irregular but continuous sounds, traveling through the air, high above us, or striking the ground in front and ricocheting over us to be imbedded in some object to the rear; others strike the wall, scattering the stones around. The fire of all those batteries seems to be concentrated on Cemetery Ridge, part of which was held by this regiment. (Before long Brown and Cushing guns were) almost completely silenced their guns being dismounted, caissons exploding, battery wagons, forges, etc., swept away, shattered into splinters, horses disemboweled, their flesh and entrails scattered, men beheaded, limbs torn, and bodies most horribly mangled into shapeless and unrecognizable masses of human flesh."[79]

General Webb was furiously trying to replace his disabled artillery pieces and repositioning his troops for the oncoming assault. Webb's Official Records of the War of the Rebellion report stated, "By 2.45 o'clock had silenced the Rhode Island battery and all the guns but one of Cushing's battery, and had plainly shown by his concentration of fire on this and the Third Brigade that an important assault was to be expected.

"I had sent, at 2 p.m., Captain Banes, assistant adjutant-general of the brigade, for two batteries to replace Cushing's and Brown's. Just before the assault, Captain Wheeler's (Cowan's)—battery, First New York Artillery (First New York Independent Battery), had gotten in position on the left, in the place occupied by the Rhode Island battery, which had retired with a loss of all its officers but one."[80]

Colonel Norman J. Hall, commander of the 3rd Brigade of the 2nd Division of Second Corps was positioned to the left of General Webb's Philadelphia Brigade and witnessed the severe shelling. His report in the Official Records of the War of the Rebellion reported:

Nothing more than occasional skirmishing occurred until the afternoon of the 3d. At 1 o'clock the enemy opened with artillery upon that portion of the line between the cemetery and the right of the Fifth Corps, several hundred yards from Round Top. The number of pieces which concentrated their fire upon this line is said to have been about one hundred and fifty. The object was evidently to destroy our batteries and drive the infantry from the slight crest which marked the line of battle, while the concentration of fire upon the hill occupied by the Second and the right of the Third Brigades indicated where the real attack was to be made. The experience of the terrible grandeur of that rain of missiles and that chaos of strange and terror-spreading sounds, unexampled perhaps, in history, must ever remain undescribed, but can never be forgotten by those who survived it.

I cannot suffer this opportunity to pass without paying just tribute to the noble service of the officers and men of the batteries that were served within my sight. Never before during this war were so many batteries subjected to so terrible a test. Horses, men, and carriages were piled together, but the fire scarcely slackened for an instant so long as the guns were standing.

Lieutenant Cushing, of Battery A, Fourth U.S. Artillery, challenged the admiration of all who saw him. Three of his limbers were blown up and changed with the caisson limbers under fire. Several wheels were shot off his guns and replaced, till at last, severely wounded himself, his officers all killed or wounded, and with but cannoneers enough to man a section, he pushed his gun to the fence in front, and was killed while serving his last canister into the ranks of the advancing enemy.

Knowing that the enemy's infantry would attack soon, I sent Lieutenant (William R.) Driver, acting assistant adjutant-general, to the Artillery Reserve for batteries, with orders to conduct them to the crest, if they were granted, with all possible speed. He arrived with one, which, though too late for service in arresting the advance of the enemy, yet had the opportunity to do him much damage.[81]

* * *

The Confederate soldiers were preparing to step off of Seminary Ridge in the midst of the worst heat of that July in Gettysburg. Professor Michael Jacobs of Pennsylvania College kept a detailed record of the weather for that fateful day. Jacobs recorded the temperature was 87 degrees at 2:00 p.m.

The Confederate shelling ceased almost as quickly as it began. An officer in the 69th Pennsylvania reported seeing three lines of Rebel troops emerging from the woods of Seminary Ridge.

Captain Haskell wrote, "There was a pause between acts, with the curtain down, soon to rise upon the great final act and catastrophe of Gettysburg."[82]

Chapter 6

WORTH A MAN'S WHILE TO SEE

THE CONSTANT SHELLING inflicted death and destruction on the opposing armies for more than an hour before the Union artillery's rate of fire slowed and then ceased, followed by the Rebel guns. Silence did not quite take over the field as the cries of the wounded and the hurried orders issued by officers filled the ears of the soldiers. As 3:00 p.m. approached on July 3, 1863, a light wind began clearing the smoke that had filled the valley between the two ridges that sheltered the armies. As the smoke slowly drifted away from the field, the Southern soldiers could see the ground before them. Presently, they would have to cross the field devoid of cover to assault the Union defenders. The Philadelphia Brigade and other Union soldiers could see the long lines of Confederate soldiers about to attack their thinly held defensive line.

The peaceful interlude Captain Frank Haskell described was soon broken. "None on that crest now need to be told that the enemy is advancing." Haskell wrote. "Every eye could see his legions, an overwhelming, resistless tide of an ocean of armed men, sweeping upon us! . . . Right on they move, as with one soul, in perfect order, without impediment of ditch, or wall, or stream, over ridge and slope, through orchard, and meadow, and cornfield, magnificent, grim, irresistible."[83]

The battle of Gettysburg now rested on the shoulders of the infantry. Haskell continued, "Word is given that the enemy is advancing. Every eye could see his legions, an overwhelming, resistless tide of an ocean of armed men, seeping upon us! Regiment after regiment and brigade after brigade, move from the woods and rapidly take their places in the lines forming the assault. . . . More than half a mile their front extends; more than a thousand yards the dull gray masses deploy, man touching man, rank pressing rank, and line supporting line. The red flags wave, their horsemen gallop up and down; . . . Gibbon rode down the line and said, 'Do not hurry, men, and fire too fast; let them come up close before you fire, and then aim low and steadily.'"[84]

Directly in the line of the Confederate assault was the 14th Connecticut infantry. Private Joseph Pierce recalled, "As far as the eye could reach could be seen the advancing troops, their war flags fluttering in the gentle summer breeze, while their sabers and bayonets flashed and glistened in the midday sun . . . the line moving forward like a victorious giant, confident of power and victory."[85] Pierce would survive the giant's charge but 68 members of his unit would fall as casualties during the three days at Gettysburg. Pierce's performance at Gettysburg earned him a promotion to corporal.

General Alexander Webb and the officers of his Philadelphia Brigade also watched the advancing Confederate giant and braced for the assault. Colonel Dennis O'Kane of the 69th Pennsylvania took a position at the stone wall and turned to address his unit. "Men, the enemy is coming . . . I know that you are as brave as any troops that you will face, but today you are fighting on the soil of your own state, so I expect you to do your duty to the utmost."[86]

O'Kane did more than expect his men to do their duty; his expectations included dying if necessary. He added, "If any man among you should flinch from that duty, I would ask the man next to him to kill him on the spot. And let your work this day be for victory or to the death."[87]

Next O'Kane unsheathed his sword, swished the weapon above his head and replaced the sword in its sheath. He then ordered his color bearers to unfurl the national flag and his own regiment's green flag that sported a gold harp on one side to honor the Irish members of the 69th Pennsylvania and the Pennsylvania coat of arms on the other to identify the unit's state.

O'Kane even invoked a famous command issued during the American Revolution during the fighting around Boston at Breed's Hill. O'Kane ordered his men to hold their fire until the enemy was close enough to see the "whites of their eyes." The order was more bravado than a military command. Union infantry would pour deadly fire into the Southern soldiers long before they could distinguish their foes' eye color. Webb had instructed his men not to fire until the enemy had crossed the Emmitsburg Road.

Webb and O'Kane cautioned and encouraged the soldiers of the Philadelphia Brigade as the Southern men that made up the units of Pickett's Charge stepped out of the woods on Seminary Ridge and took their first strides towards the Union line. O'Kane addressed each of the companies of the

69th Pennsylvania as Webb took a position on the left flank of his brigade and told his men that if they performed as they had the previous day he would be satisfied.

The encouragement by Webb and O'Kane was not necessary, according to Lieutenant Anthony McDermott of the 69th Pennsylvania. He wrote after the war all of the soldiers in the regiment believed they had more courage to meet the enemy at Gettysburg than upon any field of the war. The stimulus, according to McDermott, was the fact the troops were fighting on their own soil of Pennsylvania.

For some Union soldiers the Southern infantry attack was favored over the thundering fire of the Southern artillery pieces. McDermott wrote, "Their appearance was truly a relief from that terrible fire of their artillery. It requires less nerve to face the enemy man-to-man, in open field, than to lie down supinely while he hurls his missiles. There may be less danger in the latter process, but testimony of all gives preference to the former."[88]

To McDermott and the Union defenders, the Confederate attacking force seemed to be in perfect formation and oblivious to the danger awaiting them. McDermott wrote that "no holiday display seemed more imposing, nor troops on parade more regular, than this division of Pickett's Rebels, as they came steadily, arms at a trail."[89]

One soldier wrote of the sight of the oncoming Confederates, "Beautiful, gloriously beautiful did this vast array appear in the lovely little valley."[90] Another member of the Philadelphia Brigade recorded, "It was the grandest spectacle, the most imposing and gallant charge of the war."

Pickett's Charge was led by Southern officers, some walking and others on horseback, but all bravely leading their men. The Union men could see the swords of the Southern officers lifted towards the heavens and the sun glistening off the polished metal. The Rebel battle flags must have given the scene the look of one big festive parade. For the men of both sides the next hour would not be remembered with any delight and joy as military parades usually engender.

* * *

General John Gibbon commanded the Second Corps and had approximately 7,000 troops to fend off the attack of the approximately 12,000 Confederate troops. Gibbon was not surprised that his force would be the target of General Robert E. Lee's charge. The previous night, at the meeting of the Union generals, several of General George Gordon Meade's officers predicted Lee would attack the center of the Union defenses. The extended bombardment confirmed the Union brain trust's assessment that they were correct. Lee would attack the line's center at the Angle held by the Philadelphia Brigade and other units under Gibbon's command.

The Angle is so named as a sharp corner of a stone fence forms an angle. General Webb adjusted his units as best he could, including the remains of Battery A, 4th United States Artillery under the command of young Lieutenant Alonzo Cushing. One or two guns, conflicting reports exist of the exact number, of Cushing's battery were still operating after the Confederate bombardment. Cushing received permission to remain with his command even though Cushing was suffering from severe wounds received during the Confederate shelling.

Cushing commanded only a few gunners for his working guns. The young officer received permission from General Webb to place an artillery piece at the Angle. Extra canister rounds were placed near each gun. Also, members of the 71st Pennsylvania were on hand to man the cannons. The placement of Cushing's battery made sense but Webb would have second thoughts when the Rebels broke his line.

Lieutenant Colonel Frederick Fuger was at the Angle and recorded the conversation between Webb and Cushing. Fuger reported, "Webb came to Cushing and said, 'Cushing, it is my opinion that the Confederate infantry will now advance and attack our position.' Cushing then said, 'I had better run my guns right up to the stone fence and bring all of my canister along side each piece.'" Gen. Webb said, 'All right, do so.' . . . When enemy was within 450 yards Battery A fired with single charges of canister. At that time Cushing was wounded in the right shoulder and within a few seconds after that he was wounded in the testicles, very severe and painful wounds. He called me and told me to stand by him so that I would impart his orders to the battery: he became very ill and suffered frightfully. I wanted him to go to the rear. 'No,' he said, 'I stay right here and fight it out or die in the attempt.'"[91]

General Webb commanded the Philadelphia Brigade for less than a week. Despite his inexperience with the unit,

Webb carefully and skillfully placed his men, fewer than 1,000, along the stone wall. General Gibbon's confidence in Webb handling the sometimes undisciplined units was growing. Gibbon wrote, "Webb has taken hold of his Brigade with a will and comes down on them with a heavy hand and will no doubt soon make a great improvement."[92] By the end of the day Gibbon would have full confidence in Webb's ability.

Webb had placed the 69th Pennsylvania at the stone wall and he directed at least eight companies of the 71st Pennsylvania to extend the line. The 72nd Pennsylvania and the remaining men of the 106th Pennsylvania formed a second line on a crest of a ridge behind the Angle. To Webb's left was Colonel Norman J. Hall's brigade of the 59th New York 7th Michigan and 20th Massachusetts regiments. Hall kept the 19th Massachusetts and 42nd New York in reserve. Extending the line to Hall's left was General William Harrow's brigade that consisted of the 82nd New York, 19th Maine, 15th Massachusetts and 1st Minnesota infantry regiments.

General Alexander Hay's three brigades were to Webb's right but not connected to the 71st Pennsylvania. Near the crest of the ridge was Colonel Thomas A. Smyth's brigade that included the 14th Connecticut, 1st Delaware, 12th New Jersey and 108th New York regiments.

* * *

Before the Confederates began their deadly march across the Pennsylvania farm field, members of the Union army were unsure if they could stop the Rebel charge. One artillery man wrote, "Knowing that we had but one thin line of infantry to oppose them, I thought that our chances for Kingdom Come, or Libby Prison were very good."[93] Libby Prison was a Confederate prisoner of war facility in Richmond, Virginia.

Webb and his fellow commanders were making every preparation they could for the coming fight. Alexander Hays was on Webb's right and Hays packed the men of his two brigades tightly together, a tactic that would help thwart the charge by Confederate General James Johnston Pettigrew's men.

One member of the 20th Massachusetts, Captain Henry Abbott, had little doubt a Union victory was at hand. His unit had suffered more than 150 casualties at Fredericksburg and Abbott believed the North was about to turn the tables on the South. Abbott said Pickett's Charge was a "magnificent sight. The moment I saw them, I knew we should give them Fredericksburg. So did everybody."[94]

Abbott looked at the long lines of Confederate infantry as the soldiers steadily advanced through Union artillery fire. The shells killed and wounded scores of Southern soldiers but the survivors continued to advance. The persistence of the Southern troops was viewed with admiration by many of those under the command of Union General Winfield Scott Hancock. While the Northern troops viewed Pickett's Charge with respect, the Union soldiers weren't about to break and run, even after being subjected to the Southern bombardment.

The lack of experienced artillerymen to man the guns in

the midst of the Philadelphia Brigade proved deadly for the North. As the Confederates came close to the Emmitsburg Road, one gun crew composed mostly of infantry fired too soon, before all of the Union men were clear of the artillery piece. "The blast of canister blew the heads off (privates) Christian Rohlfing and Edward Head ."[95]

The five guns of Captain Andrew Cowan's 1st New York Independent Battery were placed behind two companies of the 59th New York and south of the copse of trees. Cowan's sixth artillery piece was placed to the north of the copse of trees.

Colonel Norman Hall noted in his Official Records of the War of the Rebellion report, "Knowing that the enemy's infantry would attack soon, I sent Lieutenant (William R.) Driver, acting assistant adjutant-general, to the Artillery Reserve for batteries, with orders to conduct them to the crest, if they were granted, with all possible speed. He arrived with one, which, though too late for service in arresting the advance of the enemy, yet had the opportunity to do him much damage."

"At 3 o'clock exactly the fire of the enemy slackened, and his first line of battle advanced from the woods in front in beautiful order. About 100 yards in rear came a second line, and opposite the main point of attack was what appeared to be a column of battalions. The conformation of the ground enabled the enemy, after advancing near the lines, to obtain cover. Arrived at this point, one battalion continued to move toward the point occupied by the Second and Third Brigades of the Second Division.

The other battalions moved by the flank until completely masked by the preceding one, when they moved by the flank again, thus forming a column of regiments. The few pieces of artillery still in position were directed upon this column, while the rebel cannon again opened with shell, firing over their own troops."[96]

*   *   *

Union General Gibbon was walking with his staff when he was informed that Pickett's Charge had commenced. "I hurriedly mounted and rode to the top of the hill where a magnificent sight met my eyes. The enemy in a long grey line was marching towards us over the rolling ground in our front, their flags fluttering in the air and serving as guides to their line of battle.

"In front was a heavy skirmish line which was driving ours on a run. Behind the front line another appeared and finally a third and the whole came on like a great wave of men. Hastily telling Haskell to ride to General Meade and tell him the enemy was coming upon us in force and we should need all the help he could send us, I directed the guns of Arnold's Battery to be run forward to the wall loaded with double rounds of canister and then rode down my line and cautioned the men not to fire until the first line crossed the Emmitsburg Road. By this time the bullets were flying pretty thickly along the line and the batteries from other portions of the field had opened fire upon the moving mass in front of us."[97]

Haskell, Gibbon's aide, recounted those moments.

"There was a pause between acts, with the curtain down, soon to rise upon the great final act and catastrophe of Gettysburg. Every eye could see his legions, an overwhelming, resistless tide of an ocean of armed men, seeping upon us! Regiment after regiment and brigade after brigade, move from the woods and rapidly take their places in the lines forming the assault. . . . More than half a mile their front extends; more than a thousand yards the dull gray masses deploy, man touching man, rank pressing rank, line supporting line. The red flags wave, their horsemen gallop up and down. . . . Gibbon rode down the line and said, 'Do not hurry, men, and fire too fast; let them come up close before you fire, and then aim low and steadily.' . . . The conflict is left to the infantry alone."[98]

Gibbon's report in the Official Records of the War of Rebellion stated when the Southern artillery barrage stopped, "The enemy displayed his first line coming out of the woods, preceded by a heavy line of skirmishers, which commenced immediately to push ours back. The line moved steadily to the front in a way to excite the admiration of every one, and was followed by a second and third, extending all along our front as far as the eye could reach. Our guns were run well forward, so as to give them a good sweep over the ground, loaded with canister, and the men warned to keep well under cover, and to reserve their fire until the enemy got well within range. As the front line came up, it was met with such a withering fire of canister and musketry as soon melted it away, but still on they came from behind, pressing forward to the wall.

By this time most of our artillerymen had fallen, and but an occasional cannon shot along our part of the line interrupted the continuous rattle of musketry. The right of the enemy's line did not extend as far as the left of my division, and, while urging forward some of my left regiments to take his line in flank, I was wounded and left the field."[99]

Gibbon would not be the last general to fall during Pickett's Charge.

William Burns of the 71st Pennsylvania wrote in his diary that the charge "was a grand sight and worth a man's while to see it."[100] Colonel Richard Penn Smith of the 71st was attempting to squeeze his entire command next to the 69th Pennsylvania. Smith reported he had to deploy the right of his unit in an open field, just north of the stone wall. The regiment was in a fearfully exposed position, Smith wrote. Smith placed Lieutenant Colonel Charles Kochersperger in command of the regiment's left wing at the forward stone wall.

Members of the 71st Pennsylvania clung to the cover of the stone wall and clutched the extra weapons gathered the night before from the field of battle. Smith estimated some of his unit had a dozen weapons. After Smith had posted his two companies in the rear, he instructed Kochersperger to hold fire until the enemy had crossed the Emmitsburg Road and then to fire as fast as possible.

Colonel Smith was with General Webb at the copse of trees when Webb ordered Smith to move his men to the stone wall and place his left flank on a sapling tree. Major William S. Stockton, 21 years old, joined the soldiers running to the stretch of stone wall unoccupied to the right of the 69th Pennsylvania. Captain William Dull of Company B was wounded during the repositioning and later died of his wounds. "Smith and Stockton, who was training to be a dentist in pre-war, watched me pack artillery pieces with everything they could find, even a bayonet."[101]

The 71st Pennsylvania and the rest of the soldiers being led by General Hancock would soon put their weapons to good use. Hancock reported his observations of the beginning of Pickett's Charge in his Official Record report:

> After an hour and forty-five minutes, the fire of the enemy became less furious, and immediately their infantry was seen in the woods beyond the Emmitsburg road, preparing for the assault. A strong line of skirmishers soon advanced (followed by two deployed lines of battle), supported at different points by small columns of infantry. Their lines were formed with a precision and steadiness that extorted the admiration of the witnesses of that memorable scene. The left of the enemy extended slightly beyond the right of General Alexander Hays' division, the right being about opposite the left of General Gibbon's. Their line of battle thus covered a front of not more than two of the small and incomplete divisions of the corps. The whole attacking force is estimated to have exceeded 15,000 men.

No attempt was made to check the advance of the enemy until the first line had arrived within about 700 yards of our position, when a feeble fire of artillery was opened upon it, but with no material effect, and without delaying for a moment its determined advance. The column pressed on, coming within musketry range without receiving immediately our fire, our men evincing a striking disposition to withhold it until it could be delivered with deadly effect.

Two regiments of Stannard's Vermont Brigade (of the First Corps), which had been posted in a little grove in front of and at a considerable angle with the main line, first opened with an oblique fire upon the right of the enemy's column, which had the effect to make the troops on that flank double in a little toward their left. They still pressed on, however, without halting to return the fire. The rifled guns of our artillery, having fired away all their canisters, were now withdrawn, or left on the ground inactive, to await the issue of the struggle between the opposing infantry.

Arrived at between 200 and 300 yards, the troops of the enemy were met by a destructive fire from the divisions of Gibbon and Hays, which they promptly returned, and the fight at once became fierce and general. In front of Hays' division it was not of very long duration. Mowed down by canister from Woodruff's battery, and by the fire from two regiments judiciously posted by General Hays in his extreme front and right, and by the fire of different lines in the rear, the enemy broke in great disorder, leaving fifteen colors and nearly 2,000 prisoners in the hands of this division. Those of the enemy's troops who did not fall into disorder in front of the Third Division were moved to the right, and re-enforced the line attacking Gibbon's division. The right of the attacking line having been repulsed by Hall's and Harrow's brigades, of the latter division, assisted by the fire of the Vermont regiments before referred to, doubled to its left and also re-enforced the center, and thus the attack was in its fullest strength opposite the brigade of General Webb. This brigade was disposed in two lines. Two regiments of the brigade, the Sixty-ninth and Seventy-first Pennsylvania Volunteers, were behind a low stone wall and a slight breastwork hastily constructed by them, the remainder of the brigade being behind the crest some 60 paces to the rear, and so disposed as to fire over the heads of those in front.[102]

Despite all of the deadly efforts of the Union Artillery and Hancock's soldiers, General Robert E. Lee's forces kept pressing forward across the Gettysburg farm fields. The line of Confederates wasn't as strong or straight as it was when the soldiers stepped off from Seminary Ridge. Their losses mounted as the Southerners advanced to a rail fence in front of the Emmitsburg Road.

To achieve Lee's goal of puncturing the Union center and causing the Union forces to retreat towards Washington, the Southerners would have to get past the troublesome fence, cross the Emmitsburg Road and break the Union's defense waiting for from them behind a stone wall and copse of trees, including the determined members of Webb's Philadelphia Brigade.

Chapter 7

WHIPPED FOR GOOD

THE CONFEDERATE SOLDIERS still standing as they approached the Emmitsburg Road found sturdy rail fences deadly obstacles. The members of the Southern infantry units were forced to spend too many dear minutes clearing the wooden fences as they were exposed to the deadly fire of the Philadelphia Brigade and other units under the command of General Winfield Hancock.

Southern soldiers either climbed the fence or crowded through holes broken in the fencing. Either way, the soldiers were momentarily stationary targets for the rifles of General Alexander Webb's men and the nearby Union artillery. The valiant Pickett's Charge was rapidly unraveling as the Southerners paid dearly to lessen the distance between them and their Northern foes. Despite the best efforts of General Hancock's corps, the Southerners continued their assault.

Members of the 71st Pennsylvania manning some of the Union artillery pieces were told to fire at the Rebels as they were climbing the fences. The command was followed and Colonel Richard Penn Smith of the 71st Pennsylvania recalled a frightful scene where havoc was caused by overloaded guns scattering deadly missiles at close range to the enemy.

Union General John Gibbon wrote, "The Southerners reached the Emmitsburg Road and began to leap over the stout fences. The column pressed on coming within musketry range without receiving immediately our fire, our men (determined) to withhold it until it could be delivered with deadly effect."[103]

For the soldiers of the 69th Pennsylvania at the stone wall, the Rebels were close enough to unleash their deadly fire. Even though Colonel Dennis O'Kane wanted them to hold fire until they could see the "whites of their eyes," some companies began firing while others didn't discharge their weapons, obeying O'Kane's command.

Once the rail fences were behind them, Southern soldiers under the command of George Pickett, James Johnson Pettigrew and Isaac Trimble, rushed the Northern defenses. Some of the troops stopped about 50 yards short of the wall and opened fire directly on the position held by the 69th Pennsylvania.   The Southerners and members of the 69th Pennsylvania exchanged deadly volleys at the relatively short range. Other Rebel troops rushed towards the Angle where the 71st Pennsylvania waited to repulse them.

Members of the Philadelphia Brigade sent volley after volley into the Confederates but couldn't stymie the Southern surge to the stone wall. In the confusion, troops under Pickett and Pettigrew found themselves thrown together as the combined force traded deadly fire at close range with General Webb's men.

From behind the low stone wall at the Angle, Private Anthony McDermott of the 69th Pennsylvania observed, "Our first round was fired with deliberation and simultaneously, and threw their front line into confusion, from which they quickly rallied and opened their fire upon us."[104] The Confederates drove towards the Angle even though losses mounted from the Union volleys described by McDermott. Private Thomas Montgomery of Company D of the 72nd Pennsylvania was one of those wounded. After the war he recalled, "We were located behind the clump of trees. I remember when the enemy was advancing upon the wall. When the regiment was ordered to move I wasn't with it. I was back at the spring with my canteen getting it filled. I seen them moving, got a musket and fell into line. There were then moving by the right flank and then turned to the front and began firing. We kept advancing slowly and firing and then I was wounded. I was shot through the leg. I went back to the rear."[105]

As the Confederates bravely continued their charge, companies of the 71st Pennsylvania at the wall under Lieutenant Colonel Charles Kochersperger's direction retreated towards the main body of the regiment. The departing soldiers left the right flank of the 69th Pennsylvania unsupported. Lieutenant Alonzo Cushing's remaining two cannons of his battery were supporting the Philadelphia Brigade by discharging rounds of canister into the nearby Confederates.

General Alexander Webb saw the retreating companies of his 71st Pennsylvania. The unit members ran headlong into members of the 72nd Pennsylvania and intermingled. There they stood firm and fired on the Confederates.

Webb later reported that the enemy advanced steadily to the fence, driving out a portion of the 71st Pennsylvania. A proud West Point graduate, Webb wasn't about to allow his men to flee in the face of the enemy. Webb shouted orders to his 72nd Pennsylvania unit, positioned on a ridge just to the rear of the 71st Pennsylvania. Webb planned to lead a charge of the 72nd Pennsylvania to retake the position abandoned by the companies of the 71st Pennsylvania.

The members of the 72nd Pennsylvania didn't follow Webb to the wall. Since Webb was new to the command, some may not have recognized him. A standard bearer didn't know Webb, or at least wouldn't obey Webb's command. Webb grabbed at the flag being held by the soldier and the two fought for the colors before numerous Confederate bullets killed the standard bearer. Webb continued to rally his men but some were reluctant to rush into the angle of death where hand-to-hand fighting was raging between Northern and Southern soldiers. Webb continued to the wall where the 69th Pennsylvania and the remaining companies of the 71st Pennsylvania were desperately trying to repel the Confederates.

William Burns of Company G of the 71st Pennsylvania wrote in his diary, "We went down to the fence and saw the Rebs advancing. It was a grand sight and worth a man's while to see it. The fight soon became awful. We moved the Rebs right and left but still they came on when we had to retreat. I thought it was all up with us when our General (Webb) rallied the men. He went right in front of us and led us when we gave a yell and charged on them and drove them back with great slaughter."[106]

Captain Andrew Cowan of the 1st New York Independent Battery, Artillery Brigade, Sixth Corps, also wrote about the heroics of General Webb. In a letter, Cowan wrote, "The enemy rushed forward with wild cheers, pouring their volleys and planted their colors upon the guns, just on my right. I fired canister low, and my last charge, two rounds in each of the six guns was fired when the advance of the enemy in my front was but ten yards distant, and while they had possession of our guns on the right. My last officer was shot down at my side just as I was directing men how to act when we had fired this 'last charge.'

"Gen. Webb and his officers were gallantly rallying the infantry and just in rear of the Regular Battery, had the colors of six or seven regiments and some few score of men fighting around them. I venture to say, on no field at no time during the war was more individual gallantry shown than on this occasion. As soon as my last charge was fired, my men pulled their guns by hand, rapidly as they could, back under the crest, and I moved quickly to a crest 50 yards or less farther back and opened fire with percussion shell again. The smoke lifted and revealed the remnants of the enemy's line retreating. I rapidly moved up again and from my old position engaged their batteries, which they had advanced from their front to cover the retreat."[107]

In a letter dated December 2, 1885, contained in the Bachelder Papers at the Gettysburg National Military Park, Cowan wrote, "Gen. Hunt was in my battery, when the enemy were within pistol range, I stood close to him, directing the fire of my guns, as he was busy emptying his revolver over his horse's head, at the rebels—and his horse being shot, one of my sergeants, O. R. Van Etten turned his own big bay over to the General. . . . When we took Brown's place Pickett's troops were forming, over at the Emmitsburg road. My last round of canister was used when the enemy got possession of Cushing's guns, and some were rushing to take mine. I saw one officer waving his sword and calling to his men to 'take that gun' just as I shouted the command to 'fire.' What was the result we did not halt to see, for my guns were dragged behind the crest of the hill on the instant of firing and the men were dragging them to the next knoll behind, where the limber chests that had been sent. . . . I was on the crest a moment, after my guns had been pulled back and in that instant I saw Webb behind Cushing's guns surrounded by a number of officers and men and the colors of two, or perhaps three of his regiments. A great many men and officers too were running away as fast as legs could carry them. James Plunkett, a Vermonter, attached to my battery, fought and cursed them and finally I saw him hit one fellow over the head with a coffee pot. The bottom burst and I shall never forget seeing the fellow running away with the pot, down over his head and face. Webb gallantly rallied his men, and the strength of the enemy was so nearly spent that the victory was ours."[108]

Casualties were mounting in the ranks of the 71st Pennsylvania. "Pvt. Robert F. Wallin of Co. C suffered a mortal head wound. Several received chest wounds and retired. John Stockton of Company I was hit in the left leg and struggled to the rear. George Beidelman was struck by a

Minie ball that cut both legs just above the knees. Private John C. Dyre, Co. E was struck in the head behind his left ear and fell unconscious. He recovered in a field hospital two hours later. He was deaf and permanently disabled."[109]

Members of the two retreating companies of the 71st Pennsylvania and the 72nd Pennsylvania grouped together on the ridge and fired upon the Confederates. Colonel Richard Penn Smith of the 71st Pennsylvania helped to rally the retreating units of his command. Because of the smoke and confusion, some of the shots fired found friendly Union soldiers as well as foes. During the Confederate assault, Union artillery discharges also killed members of the 69th Pennsylvania.

The remaining members of the 71st Pennsylvania at the stone wall engaged in a hand-to-hand struggle with the surging Confederates. Some of the unit members attached to the artillery pieces returned to fight the Rebels with artillery tools. Private Charles Olcott of Company E is credited by Colonel Smith with knocking down a Confederate officer with a sponge staff.

Smith recalled the firing became general and the sharp ring of musketry and roar of cannon and thunder of bursting shells made such a deafening noise that the human voice was drowned in the din. He said his boys loaded and fired as fast as they could. The air was filled with wild shouts and oaths. Smith wrote that he picked up a rifle and fired a few rounds. He thought that he could, Chinese-like, scare the Confederates with noise and might by accident hit a member of the enemy.

Battery I of the 1ˢᵗ United States Artillery was also taking a pounding by the Confederates. Lieutenant George A. Woodruff died while commanding the unit. According to the Bachelder papers, "As Longstreet's assaulting column advanced, Lt. Woodruff directed his men to man their guns to the left to give an enfilading fire, and while somewhat in front and facing his men, while the charge was being made, he was shot in the back, the ball passing through his body. He was taken temporarily to the shade of a tree in the rear, and subsequently to the little stone school house, on the cross road leading from the Taneytown road to the Baltimore Pike, where he died, regretting to the last that it should have been his fate to be shot in the back and asking of his friends that it should be no reflection upon his reputation."[110]

The Philadelphia Brigade was receiving much needed help from the Union regiments on its flanks. Two Vermont regiments, positioned south of the Angle and Webb's men, advanced to the front of the Union line, flanking the Confederate line. The Vermonters poured enfilading fire into the flank of General Kemper's Confederates that were congregating around the wall. The Southerners had options, none of them good, of fighting and dying, flinging themselves to the ground to avoid the deadly fire or fleeing back to the Emmitsburg Road through the deadly fire.

In the Official Records War of the Rebellion report filed by General George Stannard, he reported the Rebel charge was aimed at his command but the enemy diverged and the attack came to his right flank.

During this charge the enemy suffered from the fire of the Thirteenth and Fourteenth (Vermont), the range being short. At the commencement of the attack, I called the Sixteenth from the skirmish line, and placed them in close column by division in my immediate rear. As soon as the change of the point of attack became evident, I ordered a flank attack upon the enemy's column. Forming in the open meadow in front of our lines, the Thirteenth changed front forward on first company; the Sixteenth, after deploying, performed the same, and formed on the left of the Thirteenth, at right angles to the main line of our army, bringing them in line of battle upon the flank of the charging division of the enemy, and opened a destructive fire at short range, which the enemy sustained but a very few moments before the larger portion of them surrendered and marched in--not as conquerors, but as captives.

I then ordered the two regiments into their former position. The order was not filled when I saw another rebel column charging immediately upon our left. Colonel Veazey, of the Sixteenth, was at once ordered to attack it in its turn upon the flank. This was done as successfully as before. The rebel forces, already decimated by the fire of the Fourteenth Regiment, Colonel Nichols, were scooped almost *en masse* into our lines. The Sixteenth took in this charge the regimental colors of the Second Florida and Eighth Virginia Regiments, and the battle-flag of another regiment. The Sixteenth was supported in this new and advanced position by four companies of the Fourteenth, under command of Lieutenant-Colonel Rose.

The movements I have briefly described were executed in the open field, under a very heavy fire of shell, grape, and musketry, and they were performed with the promptness and precision of battalion drill. They ended the contest in the center and substantially closed the battle. Officers and men behaved like veterans, although it was for most of them their first battle, and I am content to leave it to the witnesses of the fight whether or not they have sustained the credit of the service and the honor of our Green Mountain State.[111]

General Gibbon wrote about the Confederate assault and his actions during Pickett's Charge.

The front line reached the Emmitsburg Road and hastily springing over the two fences, paused a moment to reform and then started up the slope. My division, up to this time, had fired but little but now from the low stone wall on each side of the angle every gun along it sent forth the most terrific fire. From my position on the left I could see the terrible effect of this. Mounted officers in the rear were seen to go down before it and as the rear lines came up and clambered over the fences, men fell from the top rails, but the mass still moved on up to our very guns and the stone wall in front.

I noticed after all three lines closed up, that the men on the right of the assaulting force were continually closing in to their left, evidently to fill the gaps made by our fire and that the right of their line was hesitating behind the clump of bushes where I had stood during the cannonade. To our left of this point was a regiment of our division and desirous of aiding in the desperate struggle now taking place on the hill to our right, I endeavored to get this regiment to swing out to the front, by a change front forward on the right company, take the enemy's line in flank to sweep up along the front of our line. But in the noise and turmoil of the conflict it was difficult to get my orders understood. Few unacquainted with the rigid requirements of discipline and of how an efficient military organization must necessarily be a machine which works at the will of one man as completely as a locomotive obeys the will of the engineer . . . in everything which the locomotive was built to obey, can appreciate the importance of drill and discipline in a crisis like the one now facing us.

In my eagerness to get the regiment to swing out and do what I wanted, I spurred my horse in front of it and waved forward the left flank. I was suddenly recalled to the absurd position I had assumed by the whole regiment opening fire! I got to the rear as soon as possible. I galloped back to my own division and attempted to get the left of that to swing out. Whilst so engaged I felt a stinging blow apparently behind the left shoulder.

I soon began to grow faint from the loss of blood which was trickling from my left hand. I directed Lt. Moale, my aide, to turn over the command of the division to General Harrow and in company with another staff officer, Captain Francis Wessells, 106th Pennsylvania, (I) left the field, the sounds of the conflict on the hill still ringing in my ears.[112]

General Hancock wrote about the wounds Gibbon received and also his wound in his Official Records of the War of the Rebellion report. "Toward the close of the main contest, I had the misfortune to lose the valuable services of a distinguished officer, Brig. Gen. John Gibbon, commanding Second Division, who was severely wounded. A short time afterward I was myself wounded, but was enabled to remain on the field until the action was entirely over, when I transferred the command to Brigadier-General Caldwell."[113]

Colonel Wheelock Veazey of the 16th Connecticut moved his men to the left of the center of the Union line after dueling with Rebel skirmishers and was present when General Hancock was wounded. Hancock was giving orders to an officer in the 13th Vermont when he received a wound in his groin. Vermont soldiers helped Hancock dismount and stretched him on the ground. Veazey reported Hancock refused to be taken from the field. As Veazey formed his men to meet the Southerners, Hancock said, "That's right, colonel, go in and give 'em hell on the flank."[114]

At the wall just north of the copse of trees, 22-year-old Lieutenant Alonzo Cushing took his last breath manning his guns. Youthful Cushing, just two years after graduating from West Point, was born in Wisconsin and grew up in New York. He would die on the field at Gettysburg. When

Cushing positioned his guns at the Angle, he became the focal point of the Confederate assault. As the Rebels were about to breach the stone wall, Cushing was preparing for his final act. "I will give them one more shot," Cushing said before he was shot through the mouth, killing him.

Lieutenant Anthony McDermott of the 69th Pennsylvania recalled in a letter to Colonel John B. Bachelder on June 2, 1886, "Poor Cushing was struck in the thighs. . . . During all that terrible storm of artillery, Cushing stood at the wall with one company, glass in hands, watching the effect of each shot from his own guns, all his demands were distinctly heard by our men. He would shout back to his men to elevate or depress their pieces so many degrees, his last command, that we heard, was 'that's excellent, keep that range.' A few moments after we were rising from the ground to receive the advancing infantry, one of our men called out 'that artillery officer has his legs knocked from under him,' thus ended the life of as cool and brave an officer as the army was possessed of."[115]

Frederick Fuger was a sergeant serving with Cushing during Pickett's Charge. Fuger, who later became a lieutenant colonel and is said to have participated in more than 60 engagements, wrote about his commanding officer's death and the fighting at the Angle.

When the enemy was within 450 yards, Battery A fired with single charges of canister. At that time Cushing was wounded in the right shoulder and within a few seconds after that he was wounded in the testicles, very severe and painful wounds. He called me and told me to stand by him so that I would impart his orders to the battery. He became very ill and suffered frightfully. I wanted him to go to the rear. 'No,' he said, 'I stay right here and fight it out or die in the attempt.'

When the enemy got within 200 yards double and treble charges of canister were used. These charges opened immense gaps in the Confederate lines to the extent of the front of a company. Lt. Milne, who commanded the right half of the battery, was killed when the enemy was within 200 yards. When the enemy was within 100 yards, Lt. Cushing was shot through the mouth and killed instantly. When I saw him fall forward I caught him with my arms and ordered several men to take his body to the rear.

That placed me in command of the battery and I announced to the men to obey my order. We still fired canister double and treble charges, but still the Confederates came on. Owing to the dense smoke I could not see very far to the front but to my utter astonishment and surprise I saw (Confederate General) Armistead leap over the stone wall with about 200 men, landing right in the midst of our battery; but my devoted cannoneers and drivers stood their ground, fighting hand-to-hand with pistols, sabers, hand spikes and rammers, until the enemy was driven out of the battery by Gen. Webb's brigade and Pickett's column collapsed. Gen. Armistead fell a few yards of where Cushing fell.

It has been asked, what other than Southern troops

would have made that charge? Ay, sir: but what other
than Northern troops would have met and repulsed it?[116]

Fuger detailed the losses suffered by Battery A at Gettysburg. He reported 83 of 90 horses were lost, "not a sound
wheel was left" on the artillery carriages, nine ammunition
chests blew up; two officers were killed, one wounded,
seven enlisted men killed, and 38 wounded. The unit had
91 men to begin July 3.

As for his commander, Fuger wrote, "Lt. Cushing was
an able soldier, distinguished for his excellent judgment and
firmness in execution and his love for the profession."[117]

Chaos took hold of the ground inside the stone wall as
Confederates gained entrance. The Southerners were led
by General Lewis Armistead pointing the way with his
hat skewered on his sword. This was the moment General
Webb was convinced a Confederate victory was imminent
and the loss would be his fault. As he later wrote his wife,
Webb wanted a bullet to end his life.

Webb wrote about the moment the Southerners swept
over the wall, "General Armistead passed over the fence
with probably over 100 of his command and several battle
flags. The 72nd Pennsylvania Volunteers were ordered up
to hold the crest and advanced to within forty paces of the
enemy's line. The 69th Pennsylvania and most of the 71st
Pennsylvania, even after the enemy were in their rear, held
their position." Webb rushed to join the 69th Pennsylvania
as his honor was saved by the heroics of his men and other
Union regiments. During the fighting, Webb was wounded

in his thigh and groin by a bullet but he wouldn't relinquish his command.

After the war, Webb wrote a letter that is contained in the files of the Gettysburg National Military Park. According to Webb, "General Armistead, an old army officer, led his men, came over my fences and passed me with four of his men. He fell mortally wounded. I got but one shot grazing my thigh. I stood about thirty-nine paces from them; their officers point me out, but God preserved me. As soon as I got my regiment up to the stone wall the enemy was whipped for good and all.

"When they came over the fences the Army of the Potomac was nearer being whipped than it was at any time of the battle. When my men fell back I almost wished to get killed. I was almost disgraced, but Hall (Colonel) on my left saw it all and brought up two regiments to help me. I would add at this moment that the word 'disgraced' was used here because I had felt that where I had put Cushing I should have gone myself and wanted the support to take the place where I had placed him."[118]

❊ ❊ ❊

Colonel Arthur J. Devereux of the 19th Massachusetts, in a document contained in the Bachelder papers, described his unit's actions on July 3, 1863, and the thin Union defense that opposed Pickett.

There was but one line of infantry from the left up to Webb's position where one of his regiments was retired a few paces. One spirited writer has fixed the immortal stamp upon that 'Single Line of Blue.' . . . The division laid there on its arms. The calm resting over all, scarcely any movement making itself apparent to disturb the universal hush. Suddenly a single gun from the enemy's lines broke the oppressive stillness. It was plainly a signal. No sooner had its report roused the attention that every gun on Seminary Ridge opens in one grand salvo with concentric fire on Gibbon's division. . . . The firing of cannon ceased almost as suddenly as it began and Pickett's splendid division moved out to cross the (field) between the two low lying ridges occupied by the opposing armies, on that magnificent charge which has extorted the admiration, unqualified, of their foes, must be memorable in history. . . .

Today the Nineteenth Mass., has with it the Forty-second New York, Tammany's contribution to the country's cause. . . . Col. (James) Mallon and myself could view the whole scene standing up as we were and were probably the only persons close enough readily to distinguish all which occurred and so entirely free from personal participation as to be able intelligently to judge it. We see that Webb cannot firmly hold his men against the shock of that fierce charge through he may throw himself with reckless courage in front to fact the storm and beg, threaten and command. Hall's right overlapped, has to sag back with sullen fury, swaying to the rear from the pressure . . . A great gap yarns, immediately between Webb and Hall. The entire width of the Oak

Grove and for some distance to the right is stripped of defense of our line.

Every gun on our front is silenced. Woodruff, Cushing, Brown, Rorty and every other commissioned officer, almost without exception, of the respective batteries is dead or disabled and Gibbon badly wounded. 'Mallon we must move.' Just then a headlong rush of horse's feet spurred to the utmost, came up the hollow behind me from the direction of the Baltimore Pike. I turned. There, looking the very embodiment of the god of war rode Hancock, the 'Superb.' (Devereux sought and received permission from Hancock to enter the fight.) He (Hancock) shot like an arrow past my left toward Hall's struggling lines receiving in a few seconds the wound that swept him from his saddle and so nearly cost him his life.

In the meanwhile Mallon, springing from my side was instantly with his men and both regiments on the double quick moved side by side to fill that fearful gap. The two lines came together with a shock which stopped both and caused a slight rebound. For several minutes they faced and fired into each other at a distance (which I carefully measured after the fight) a little short of fifteen paces. Everything seemed trembling in the balance. Whichever side could get a motion forward must surely win. . . . The opposing lines were standing as if rooted, dealing death into each other, how long it is impossible to say with exactness. There they stood and wouldn't move. . . . Our line seemed to actually leap forward. There was at once an indescribable rush of quick hurrying scenes ... My line seemed to open as if by magic. It was not flight however, a flood of unarmed, defenseless men poured through. They almost ran over me. The remnant of Pickett's gallant men abandon that early invincible charge and Gettysburg translated, reads A Nation Saved.[119]

Devereux concluded that if the Union line had failed, Lee's plan would have succeeded and the South would have been recognized by foreign powers.

* * *

Joseph R. C. Ward, who wrote the *History of the 106th Pennsylvania* in 1883, reported the 106th did follow Webb to the wall. "Capt. Lynch said, 'General, the One Hundred and Sixth is with you,' and with those of the 69th that joined them. Capt. Sperry advanced, passing the left of the 72nd, now inspired by the personal gallantry of General Webb, who, with sword in hand, called upon them to follow him, and they rushed upon the enemy now advancing towards the crest; from the right, came the 71st, from the front, the 72nd, and from the left, the battalion of the 106th together, driving them back over the fence. . . . at the same time Col. Hall came to Webb's aid."[120]

Armistead urged his men to follow him and to give the Union soldiers the "cold steel" of their bayonets. Actually, no wounds from "cold steel" were reported by Union troops. Once inside the Union defense, Armistead ran to one of the abandoned guns of Cushing's battery. Armistead was cut down by Union fire and once his presence was eliminated, the Confederate charge lost some of its momentum. Rebels did continue the assault and some ran to the dense copse of trees, a place later called the "High Water Mark of the Confederacy."

Colonel Richard Penn Smith called Armistead a brave man in a letter he wrote to a fellow officer.

* * *

Before the Civil War while both served in the United States military, Union General Winfield S. Hancock and Confederate General Lewis Armistead were close associates. They both became casualties during Pickett's Charge. On January 5, 1869, Captain Henry H. Bingham, aide to Hancock, wrote a letter to Hancock concerning the death of Armistead and the wounding of Hancock and also a controversial message he relayed to Hancock from Armistead.

Bingham wrote, "I saw Armistead first at the high point of the enemy's repulse. I was on the right and alongside of Webb's brigade, second line, just at the crest, when Webb's front line was driven back. I was wounded and did all I could to rally the troops, my horse was wounded but not seriously. I met Armistead just under the crest of the hill, being carried to the rear by several privates. Privates thought it was Longstreet. I dismounted from my horse and inquired of the prisoner his name, he replied General Armistead of the Confederate Army. Observing that his suffering was very great I said to him, 'General I am Captain Bingham of General Hancock's staff and if you have anything valuable in your possession which you desire taken care of, I will take care of it for you.' He then asked me if it was General Winfield Scott Hancock and upon my replying in the affirmative he informed me that you were an old and valued friend of his and that he desired me to say to you 'Tell Gen. Hancock for me that I have done him and done you all an injury which I shall regret or repent (I forget the exact word) the longest day I live.' I then obtained his spurs, watch, chain, seal and pocketbook. I told the men to take him to the rear to one of the hospitals.

"I was mounted when I came to you on the field where you were wounded. I was riding along the line of Webb's troops encouraging and rallying them when I met Armistead."[121]

The exact words and meaning of what Armistead told Bingham about doing Hancock and everyone an injury has been hotly disputed since the Civil War. Was Armistead attempting to ask forgiveness for joining the rebellion? That is the undecided issue.

Bingham was wounded by a spent bullet soon after the Southern artillery cannonade began on July 3. He received medical attention for his wound and then rejoined the battle and was given an order by General George G. Meade to Hancock concerning the preserving of artillery rounds for the upcoming Confederate infantry charge.

✳ ✳ ✳

The remaining members of the 69th Pennsylvania were in a desperate struggle with the Confederates in the dense thicket of the copse of trees. Southerners were shooting into the rear of the 69th as Webb's men were being hit from two directions. One report estimated 200 Confederates had reached a position to the rear of the 69th Pennsylvania. The valiant members of the Philadelphia Brigade fought for their lives and for the Union but they were in jeopardy of being overrun when aid arrived.

Colonel Norman J. Hall, stationed to the left of the Philadelphia Brigade, saw the Confederates swarm into the Angle. Hall ordered his small brigade to rush to the Pennsylvanians' aid. "The enemy was rapidly gaining a foothold," Hall reported. General Hancock arrived at Hall's side and concurred with the order to help the 69th Pennsylvania. Joined by General William Harrow's brigade, the soldiers rushed en masse past parts of the Philadelphia Brigade and into the Confederate invaders.

* * *

Captain Frank Haskell of Gibbon's staff was also looking for troops to send to help the Philadelphia Brigade. He authored a dramatic account of Gettysburg shortly after the battle concluded. "The conflict was tremendous, but I had seen no wavering in all our line," Haskell recorded. "Then saw a large portion of Webb's brigade by the group of trees and the angles of the wall, was breaking from the cover of the works, and without order or reason, with no hand uplifted to check them, was falling back, a fear-stricken flock of confusion. The fate of Gettysburg hung upon a spider's single thread!"[122]

Haskell wrote that he drew his sword, something he

never did, and ordered the men to "halt and face about and fire." They obeyed his commands, according to Haskell, as he "used the flat edge of the sword on some." He continued, "General Webb came to my assistance. He was on foot, but he was active, and did all that one could do to repair the breach or to avert its calamity. The men that had fallen back, facing the enemy, soon regained confidence and became steady. This portion of the wall was lost to us, and the enemy gained the cover of the reverse side, where he now stormed with fire. But Webb's men, with their bodies in part protected by the abruptness of the crest, now sent back in the enemy's faces as fierce a storm."[123]

Little could now be seen of the Confederates through the smoke, according to Haskell. "Webb's men were falling fast, and he is among them to direct and encourage, but however well they may now do with that walled enemy in front, with more than a dozen flags to Webb's three, it soon becomes apparent that in not many minutes they will be overpowered, or that there will be none alive for the enemy to overpower. Webb has but three regiments, all small, the 69th, 71st and 72nd Pa; the 106th except two companies not here today, and he must have speedy assistance or this crest will be lost. . . . As a last resort I resolved to see if Hall and Harrow could not send some of their commands to reinforce Webb."[124]

✻ ✻ ✻

Members of the 69th Pennsylvania later wrote they weren't sure how any of them survived the fighting at the copse of trees. One who didn't was the unit's commander, Colonel Dennis O'Kane.

As General Armistead was leading the Southerners over the stone wall, O'Kane ordered three companies of the 69th Pennsylvania to refuse the right of the line, fall back and then charge. The companies formed a right angle to the seven companies remaining at the wall to their left. The formation placed the Confederates in a cross fire. Two of the companies, A and I, complied with O'Kane's order but a third company never received its instructions as Captain George C. Thompson of Company F was shot in the head and killed before delivering the orders. Thompson's company remained at the wall, causing a gap in the line. With its flank uncovered, every member of Company F was reported to have been killed, captured or wounded.

Thompson raised a unit that became F Company, 69th Pennsylvania. Thompson's death and the undelivered orders almost collapsed the regiment.[125] Captain Thompson was a Unitarian, unlike most of the others who were Catholics in the regiment. He was twice married and 40 years old at his death, leaving a widow and four children.

Lieutenant Anthony McDermott of the 69th Pennsylvania wrote of Thompson's death in a letter to Colonel John B. Bachelder on June 2, 1886. "The troops on our right abandoned their position which left a blank space, that Armistead was quick to take advantage of. Seeing it, he rushed through his ranks, taking off his hat and putting it on the point of his sword, he raised it for a standard waving it he ran along our front to a point near the angle and crossed the wall, his men following him, then continued in the direction towards where Gen. Webb stood, when he was trying to get the 72d to come up to our assistance, the first three companies were now ordered change their front to protect our right and rear, those being 'I,' 'A' and 'F.'

"The enemy in our front was pouring in their shot, and Armistead's followers were giving it to us from our right flank. Co. I and A quickly changed and moved back to the crest to get between Armistead and Cushing's four pieces. Co. F seemed to either not have received the order in time or had no desire to leave the wall hence an opening was left which let the enemy get between them and our two flanking Cos. They rushed in on the rear of our main line, and it looked as though our regiment would be annihilated, the contest here became a hand-to-hand affair. Company F completely hustled over the stone wall into the enemy's ranks, and all were captured, their Capt. Geo. Thompson being killed, their Lt's. wounded and prisoners."[126]

O'Kane's command was quickly becoming ineffective despite individual bravery in the face of the determined Rebel assault. One of O'Kane's trusted officers, Lieutenant Colonel Martin Tschudy, was shot through the bladder and killed as the fighting at the wall became contested at close quarters with some even using their muskets as clubs.

"Cpl. Hugh Bradley of Tinen's company, who was known as 'quite a savage sort of fellow,' struck out on all sides with his musket clubbed until a Confederate crushed his skull with a musket. Bradley's was the only death in the regiment that any survivor of the 69th recalled was due to anything but musketry or artillery fire. Many men were struck by rifle barrels and butts, but few caused disabling injuries."[127]

As O'Kane was repositioning his men to close gaps, he fell victim to a Southern shot. "A Minie ball had passed through his abdomen and he was bleeding profusely. In the time that it took to get a stretcher, O'Kane drifted in and out of consciousness, but he could hear from behind the trees the volleys of the Union regiments that had moved into position on the slope above him. As he was lifted on to the stretcher, O'Kane was dimly aware that the firing had begun to diminish. 'The line held,' he thought. 'The line held.' O'Kane slipped into a coma and died during the early morning hours of July 4."[128]

With O'Kane out of action and the 69th Pennsylvania line in disarray, the Rebels attempted to exploit the gaps in the Union line. The famous Rebel yell was coming from the throats of many of the Confederate troops as they rushed to take over the remaining Union artillery pieces defending the Angle. Organization was mostly lost, Hall reported, and commands were useless in the confusion.

Rebels were urging the men of the 69th Pennsylvania to surrender but only a few heeded the suggestion. "The fighting here continued until (Confederate General James) Kemper fell, seriously wounded near our colors. . . . With Kemper's fall the enemy here surrendered," Lieutenant Anthony McDermott of the 69th Pennsylvania recorded in a letter. "We poured our fire upon (the enemy) until Armistead received his mortal wound; he swerved from

Pickett's Charge is named for Confederate General George Edward Pickett. Pickett, who was from Virginia, survived the battle and the Civil War.

General Alexander Webb commanded the Philadelphia Brigade at Gettysburg. His troops held the pivotal defensive position during Pickett's Charge. After the war, he served as president of the City College of New York.

This carte de visite (CDV) of General Alexander Webb is from the collection of author Bruce E. Mowday

The back of Webb's CDV indicates the photo was taken in New York City by C. D. Fredericks.

General George Gordon Meade commanded the Union army at Gettysburg. He took over leadership of the Army of the Potomac just days before the battle.

Union General John Gibbon commanded the Second Division of the Second Corps at Gettysburg and for a period of time commanded the Second Corps.

Confederate General Robert E. Lee commanded Southern forces at Gettysburg and was responsible for ordering the failed Pickett's Charge.

General Winfield Scott Hancock commanded the Second Corps at Gettysburg and was wounded during Pickett's Charge. He was known as "Hancock the Superb." He later ran for President of the United States and lost.

The Medal of Honor began during the Civil War period. A number of the medals were awarded for bravery at Gettysburg and especially at Pickett's Charge. This medal was designed by the Tiffany Company.

The spirit of the Union soldier at Gettysburg was captured by renowned Chadds Ford artist Karl Kuerner in this painting, *Gettysburg: A Sense of History*.

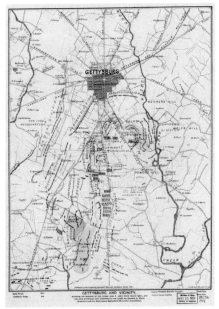

This drawing depicts Confederate Generals James Longstreet and George Pickett at the beginning of Pickett's Charge. Longstreet was opposed to the charge but followed commanding officer General Robert E. Lee's orders.

A map from the archives of the Library of Congress shows troop positions during the third day of fighting, July 3, 1863, at Gettysburg.

J. Howard Wert Illustrations

The illustrations depicted on the remaining pages are from the J. Howard Wert Gettysburg Collection™ and The American Heritage and History Virtual Museum. Many of these objects have not been made public and are part of the collection of the private museum.

J. Howard Wert was a soldier, educator and author born in Gettysburg in 1841. During the Gettysburg campaign, Wert was a special scout for the Union. Although detained by Confederate troops, he escaped and aided General Meade's Union troops.

After the battle, Wert and Frank Haskell, a member of General Gibbon's staff, rode over the battlefield. Wert began collecting items from the battle, a pastime he pursued over the years. Wert wrote a guidebook and authored other articles about the battle of Gettysburg. Noted Civil War author Ed Bears wrote, "Wert walked in the very footsteps of history . . . but most of all he was a patriot."

All these images are courtesy of the J. Howard Wert Gettysburg Collection.™

Union General Henry Slocum's campaign brief case and monogrammed pocket knife

Richmond rifled-musket, red belt and cap box, Kerr Revolver and leather holster found where Pickett's men made their charge

A round hardtack issued to Confederate troops. Hardtack was a main staple of Confederate meals and few survive. The inscription reads, "Bread from dead Virginian's bag, Gettysburg, July 5, 1863."

A picture with the inscription "Honor Our Brave Defenders of Virginia"

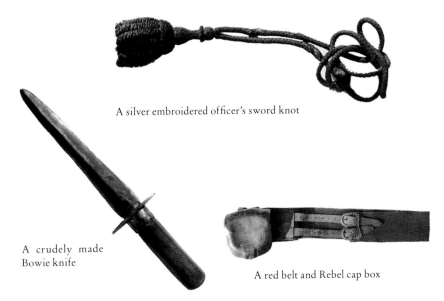

A silver embroidered officer's sword knot

A crudely made
Bowie knife

A red belt and Rebel cap box

A Rebel haversack with strap believed to have belonged to Lt. Haywood of 53rd Virginia, Company K

A framed image of Union General Winfield Scott Hancock

A framed keepsake of items belonging to Colonel Paul Joseph Revere, 20th Massachusetts, including his portrait, button, and pair of eagle shoulder straps. Revere was the grandson of Paul Revere of American Revolution fame. He died from wounds received at Gettysburg.

A side hammer Allan and Wheelock revolver

Soldiers often carried images of family members and this is a grouping of CDVs (carte de visite) from a soldier.

This image is from a solder of the 72nd Pennsylvania, a unit of the Philadelphia Brigade that defended the Angle against Pickett's soldiers. The items include a red bandana scarf and medals.

Two Philadelphia Brigade silver Masonic medals

A patriotic hymn book carried by a member of the Philadelphia Brigade

Pipe and silver match case of Colonel Joseph Barnes of the 72nd Pennsylvania

These items are connected with Colonel Joseph Barnes of the 72nd Pennsylvania, who wrote a history of the Philadelphia Brigade. Included in the grouping is a box holding a death/mourning card, red velvet fez smoking cap, holster and silver mounted revolver.

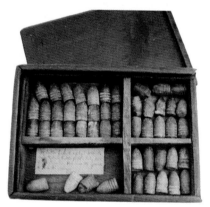

This box contains about 50 minie balls and a handwritten note by J. Howard Wert.

A relic pot with shrapnel damage from the Bryan House along with a cannon ball and minie balls. The house was owned by an African American farmer and used by Union troops near Cemetery Ridge.

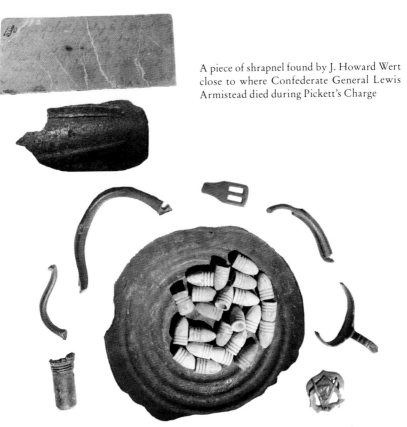

A piece of shrapnel found by J. Howard Wert close to where Confederate General Lewis Armistead died during Pickett's Charge

Half of a U.S. canteen with various relics plowed up after the war along the defensive line of the Union army during Pickett's Charge

A Pepper Box revolver found at the Angle

A damaged double-barrel pistol found immediately after the battle at the scene of Pickett's Charge

The pistol cartridge and cap box and merit Oration medal from the Virginia Military Institute carried by Colonel James K. Marshall of the 52nd North Carolina. Only one other Confederate officer's cartridge and cap box is known to exist. Marshall was related to the famous Marshall family of Virginia. He died at the Bliss Farm on July 3, 1863.

A U. S. canteen, cannon vent pick, horse bit and enlisted man's brass shoulder scale found near the location of Cushing's battery at the Angle

A grouping of relics found near Emmitsburg Road where Confederates crossed on July 3, 1863

These relics from Pickett's Charge were found more than a decade after the battle. Shown are a Tower rifle brass trigger guard fragment, brass scabbard ring, leather buckle, spoon, Colt .44 cylinder loaded with three linen cartridges, shrapnel and a fragment of a U. S. bayonet.

A red prayer book used by Confederate James Hogan of Virginia

A tin box along with an officer's gold sword tassel, Jew's harp , brass bullet mold, and image of a Rebel lost on the battlefield during Pickett's Charge

A rare Colt .31 and holster that belonged to Colonel Birkett Fry, who became a friend of J. Howard Wert

A Confederate cartridge box and cartridge wrapper made of paper

An engraving depicting the evacuation of Union wounded
during Pickett's Charge

An engraving depicting a charge by General Alexander
Webb's Philadelphia Brigade during Pickett's Charge

A proof by noted Civil War artist Charles Magnus

Oil portrait of Union General Winfield S. Hancock, one of the heroes of Gettysburg

Encased binoculars used by Union General Oliver O. Howard at Gettysburg and given to J. Howard Wert after the war

A broken beam from the Codori Barn, scene of fighting during Pickett's Charge, and a Peace rifle flash with shoulder cord

A wallet with eagle impression and photos found along the Union line at Pickett's Charge

These items are from the Codori Farm and are associated with Colonel Norman Hall's brigade. The black leather ink well was used by Hall.

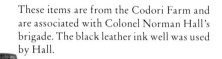

Items associated with the Philadelphia Brigade, the brigade that held the Union center during Pickett's Charge

A bandana and U. S. cartridge box plate found with the Philadelphia Brigade items

Buttons and a wood box found by J. Howard Wert. Some of the buttons are associated with the 72nd Pennsylvania Regiment.

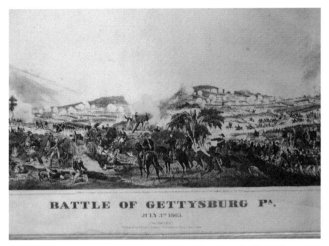

A large print of a Gettysburg rendering by famed Civil War artist Charles Magnus

A Union horse bit found near Union General George Meade's headquarters

Brass spurs found near Union General George Meade's headquarters

Fuses, fuse cutter and a reamer used by Union artillerymen

A flask carried by Colonel Addison Mason of Union General George Meade's staff

A portrait of Captain John Egan who served in Woodruff's Battery during Pickett's Charge

Double lensed sunglasses, brass eagle match safe and leather shield glass case

A pipe bowl owned by Captain J. S. Scott of the 69th Pennsylvania, who was severely wounded during Pickett's Charge

A blue cloth-covered canteen

the way in which he winced, as though he was struck in the stomach, after wincing or bending like a person with cramp, he pressed his left hand on his stomach, his sword and hat (a slouch) fell to the ground. He then made two or three staggering steps, reached out his hands trying to grasp at the muzzle of what was then the 1st piece of Cushing's battery, and fell. I was at the time the nearest person to him. At the time he was struck his fall was much the same time that Kemper fell."[129]

General Hancock in his Official Records of the War of the Rebellion report also commented on the confusion taking place on the battlefield, specifically when Webb's regiment received reinforcements from Hall's units. "The movement was executed, but not without confusion, owing to many men leaving their ranks to fire at the enemy from the breastwork. The situation was now very peculiar. The men of all the brigades had in some measure lost their regimental organization, but individually they were firm. The ambition of individual commanders to promptly cover the point penetrated by the enemy, the smoke of battle, and the intensity of the close engagement, caused this confusion. The point, however, was now covered. In regular formation our line would have stood four ranks deep."[130]

Major James Duffy was the third officer to command the 69th Pennsylvania during Pickett's Charge. Duffy, Irish born, operated Duffy's Hotel on South Broad Street, Philadelphia, before the war and the unit's sergeant-major, Michael Coyne, worked as a bartender. Duffy, who was positioned with the troops on the left flank, was wounded during the fighting as he suffered a gunshot wound to the thigh. Duffy would die from complications of his leg wound in June 1869.

The terrible losses of the 69th Pennsylvania were noted by Adjutant Anthony W. McDermott of the 69th Pennsylvania, who wrote in a unit history that the regiment lost all of its field officers in repulsing this charge—the colonel, D. O'Kane, being mortally wounded, dying a few hours after; the Lt. Col. M. Tslchudy, being killed while rallying the right to oppose Armistead. Major Duffy, was seriously wounded on the left of the line. McDermott reported the adjutant was slightly wounded near the close of the fight and four line officers killed and six wounded and the two lieutenants of Company F taken prisoners. Of the non-commissioned officers and privates, 39 killed, 80 wounded and 16 prisoners, according to McDermott.

In a letter to Colonel John Bachelder after the war that is contained in the files of Gettysburg National Military Park, McDermott added information concerning the deaths of the officers of his regiment. "Among our losses was Co. D. O'Kane, who fell like a solider in great glee because his men could not be driven from their position, he was not an educated man, and was gruff in his speech, but with all he had a heart as tender as a woman's and above all things he despised a coward. Our Lt. Col. M. Tshudy, who was killed also, fell while endeavoring to beat back the enemy who had fell upon our rear. He was a lawyer by profession, with a warm sun-shining nature, with a pleasant word for every one. He was wounded on the side of the head during the attack on our lines by Anderson's division, but refused to leave the field."[131]

The repositioning of Union forces from the stone wall necessitated a slackening of fire from the Northern defenders. Southerners continued their assault and ran through members of the 69th Pennsylvania. The fighting at the wall and near the 69th Pennsylvania colors "was more desperate than at any point of our line," McDermott recalled. "Joseph McKeever, who was within the mob of men, stated later that 'everybody was loading and firing as fast as they could,' but the Confederates came in all around them. 'How they fired without killing all our men I do not know,' he testified. 'We thought we were all gone.'"[132]

Major Samuel Roberts of the 72nd Pennsylvania wrote a letter to General Webb after the war that is contained in the Bachelder Papers at the Gettysburg National Military Park, Gettysburg. Roberts cited information from Captain Robert Steward of the 72nd Pennsylvania and Lieutenant Charles McAnally of the 69th Pennsylvania concerning the advance of Pickett's troops. "The fence on the Emmitsburg road to our left was mostly destroyed, but on our immediate front almost intact, the delay of the single brigade that moved to the left of the house was caused by forming line of battle while the two brigades that moved to the (enemy's) right of the house met with no obstruction. Stuart remained where he was wounded, the enemy passing over him, after the repulse he came into our lines." Roberts also reported that Lieutenant Charles Troutman of the 12th New Jersey reported the enemy of Heth's division commanded by

Pettigrew was within twenty feet of the Union line when the enemy broke. "Several Confederates had been struck by boulders hurled at them by some of the 12th New Jersey who either had no time to reload their pieces or were out of ammunition."[133]

Among Hall's regiments sent to support the 69th Pennsylvania was the 19th Massachusetts and 42nd New York infantry regiments. Colonel Arthur Devereux's regiment joined in the rush to the Angle. Devereux wrote that he had been "watching the course of events unable to make use of my own men up to the time when I saw that Webb could not sustain the shock with his front line."[134] General Hancock had concurred with Hall's advance and added they should do so "God damned quick."[135] Gibbons aide, Lieutenant Frank Haskell, had also urged Hall to support Webb's brigade. Haskell gave Hall a report on the engagement to that point, "Well, but Webb is hotly pressed, and must have support or will be overpowered. Can you assist him? You cannot be too quick."[136]

Colonel James E. Mallon of the 42nd New York, the Tammany Regiment, heeded Hancock's call to assist the Philadelphia Brigade and joined Devereux rush towards the Angle. The advance, according to Devereux, was a "sharp right oblique" through Cowan's battery and toward the copse of trees. Both regiments were followed by the 20th Massachusetts. One Confederate officer reported his troops were being attacked from every side in overwhelming numbers.

The 72nd Pennsylvania, positioned just to the east and rear of the 69ᵗʰ Pennsylvania, also provided valuable fire power. A newspaper article printed a month after Gettysburg on August 6, 1863, in the *Baltimore American and Commercial Advertiser* gave a first-hand account of the fighting at the Angle. The author is not identified but is apparent he is a member of Philadelphia Brigade and could have been with the 72ⁿᵈ Pennsylvania.

This was the pinch, and the officers knew it. General Gibbon had just been hit, some one said, and almost at the same time General Hancock was badly wounded, and both were taken off the field to the rear. I recollect seeing Gibbon's aide (Haskell) trying to rally the men, and do it manfully, too. He did a man's part in steadying the line. So did Webb, who was on foot in the midst of the men. Webb was everywhere. So was Colonel Smith, (71ˢᵗ Pennsylvania). At this time the enemy was crossing over the stone fence near the clumps of trees and their red flags waving, as it seemed to me, in triumph already, though (Colonel Norman) Hall was all right and his men were steady on our left. . . . by this time the officers had stopped the falling back and were driving the stragglers to the front, though we did not go forward to the stone wall, yet, but all were facing the enemy and firing heavily—not in ranks for everyone seemed going to it pretty much on his own hook, . . . We had wished for Hall, so he came as wished, and his right marked by the flank of our left and got mixed with our men. . . . Officers on both sides were using their pistols; the color sergeant of the 72nd Pa went forward with his colors, the lance of which had been shot in two. The soldiers followed with a rush; no one wanted to straggle now. The wall was gained and crossed and the work of taking prisoners commenced. Lee's great assault had failed. . . . (saw Meade talking to Haskell) and asked about assault and when told repulsed, Meade said, "I thank God," and made a motion to wave his hat, but he did not, but waved his right hand and hurrahed, while his son (Meade's aide) took off his hat and hurrahed like a good fellow. The dead men and horses were lying thick around; there was still some firing going on, and we were all—that is, all of us that were left—begrimed with powder and dust, and many were bleeding; but it was a good thing to see our General, so cool, so much at ease, and speaking such a soldierly way. The reinforcements soon came up, but we had done without them.[137]

The collapse of the Rebel charge in the front of General Alexander Hays' troops was reported by General Hancock in his Official Records of the War of the Rebellion report. Hancock wrote, "Arrived at between 200 and 300 yards, the troops of the enemy were met by a destructive fire from the divisions of Gibbon and Hays, which they promptly returned, and the fight at once became fierce and general. In front of Hays's division it was not of very long duration. Mowed down by canister from Woodruff's battery, and by the fire from two regiments judiciously posted by General Hays in his extreme front and right, and by the fire of different lines in the rear, the enemy broke in great disorder."[138]

Author David M. Jordan wrote about Hancock's actions during Pickett's Charge in his *Winfield Scott Hancock: A Soldier's Life*:

> As the Confederates moved forward, silent, without their rebel yell, Hancock was galloping back and forth along his line, making sure that everything was ready and being cheered by a couple of regiments as he passed.
>
> He noted with approval that Hays had judiciously placed two regiments on his right out in front of the general line, and he observed with interest that two regiments of George Stannard's Vermont Brigade at the left of the Second Corps line, were 'posted in a little grove of and at a considerable angle with the main line.'
>
> The Confederates came closer, and the force on Hays's right faced about to the left and shattered the brigades of Brockenbrough and Davis with an enfilading fire, effectively destroying the left of the rebel advance. On the Union left, the fire of the Vermont regiments combined with artillery fire from Little Round Top caused the Confederate right to drift toward the center—toward the 'clump of trees' which Lee had initially selected as his target. It was at about this time that Richard B. Garnett, commanding one of Pickett's brigades, was killed.
>
> Hancock, meanwhile, galloped over to Stannard to have his Vermonters make a flanking attack. Hancock had just given some directions to Colonel Randall of the

13th Vermont when a rebel ball tore into his groin. The Vermonters assisted the stricken general from his horse and stretched him out on the ground. Hancock insisted that he remain there until the battle was over, and he propped himself up on one elbow to watch its progress.

As Hancock watched, Colonel Wheelock G. Veazey, an old friend and now commander of the 16th Vermont, passed by. Hancock called him over, grasped his hand, and cried, 'Go in, Colonel, and give it to them on the flank.' In the Vermonters went, and with Hall, and Webb, and Harrow, and with all the common soldiers who had rushed to close up the break in the Union line, they shattered the 'High Water Mark of the Confederacy,' as Armistead's penetration has long been called. The great assault was over, Pickett's charge had failed, and Gettysburg was a Union victory.[139]

The combined fire power of the massing Union troops blunted the Confederate surge. Since Rebel General Robert E. Lee had not sent supporting troops to exploit the hole punctured in the Union center, the Southerners had no option but end Pickett's Charge in defeat. Lee, who left the planning of the details to General James Longstreet, had lost his attempt to dislodge the Army of the Potomac. As the Rebels retreated, additional Northern units rushed to the wall to support the Philadelphia Brigade, but most arrived after the Rebels were moving back through the farm fields where less than an hour before they had proudly marched towards the forces of Meade, Hancock, Gibbon and Webb.

Chapter 8

FIERCEST BATTLE EVER FOUGHT

L ARGE SEGMENTS OF General Alexander Webb's Philadelphia Brigade held their original positions as the fight drained out of the few Southerners remaining inside the confines of the stone wall. Retreating, retracing their way back across the field where the historic charge took place, the remaining Rebel troops fled. Gettysburg was a great Northern victory. The Union was saved from secession.

For General Webb, he was far from being disgraced. Webb was a Civil War hero who earned a Medal of Honor for his heroism at the Angle.

William J. Burns of Company G of the 71st Pennsylvania wrote in his diary about some of the "shocking sights" he saw after the battle concluded. "After the fight I went over the battlefield. It was very thick with dead and wounded Rebs. Brought in the wounded and lay at the fence all night." The sight was terrible to behold as dismembered bodies were strewn across the landscape and wounded begged for help or to be put out of their misery.

A regimental history of the 71st Pennsylvania noted the members scarcely given way to a feeling of exultation over the victory. The members were filled with sadness at the evidence, on every hand, of the terrible sacrifice of life with which it had been purchased. Dead bodies of Rebels were stretched across bodies of wounded Federals. Wounded were struggling to escape dead comrades next to them. The crippled and dead artillery horses lay scattered upon the field. A multitude of disabled artillery, muskets, canteens, knapsacks, all the munitions of war, were thick on the field. The regiment buried these on the spot where they fell, and at one end of the huge grave a board was placed bearing the inscription the remains of the Ninth and Seventeenth Virginia, Regiments. A worthy foe.

Death and suffering wasn't confined to humans, as a large number of horses were also casualties at Gettysburg.

The day after the battle Colonel Charles Wainwright wrote, "There was about an acre or so of ground where you could not walk without stepping over the bodies, and I saw perhaps a dozen cases where they were heaped one on top of the other."[140]

More than the dead and wounded were gathered from the ground around the copse of trees. As the firing subsided, victorious Union soldiers gathered trophies; such as flags, swords, rifles, pistols and other military accoutrements.

General George Meade arrived on the scene just as the last of the survivors of Pickett's Charge retreated. He wrote in a letter that "Captain Haskell of Gibbon's staff" was the only officer he recognized and asked if the enemy had been defeated.[141]

Meade is quoted as saying, "Thank God," and then a hoarse "Hurrah!" as he watched a group of Southern prisoners being marched to the rear.[142] For many of the Northern soldiers, especially those in the Second Corps, the repulse of Pickett's Charge was a revenge for losses suffered during the fighting at Fredericksburg. During the December 1862 battle, Union forces suffered more than 12,000 casualties, including more than 1,200 killed.

Meade's son, Captain George Meade, wrote a letter to John Bachelder on May 6, 1882, that is contained in the Bachelder Papers at the Gettysburg National Military Park. The letter gives information as Pickett's Charge was concluding. "When I rode alongside of the Gen. (Meade) he turned to me and smiling said 'Hello George, is that you. I am glad you are here, you must stick by me now, you are the only officer left,' and then added something about its being a pretty lively place. He then said, 'Lets go up here and find out what is going on.'"[143] Captain Meade also wrote about prisoners being directed to the rear for safety. "Almost at once the enemy's batteries opened and their shells commenced falling all around and these prisoners scampered off cheering. I remember some of the shouting, 'Why it's hotter here than it was in the front.' In less space of time than it has taken me to write this, there was not a Confederate to be seen.' About this time, according to Captain Meade, was when Haskell met with his father, General Meade.

Meade was victorious in his first battle as commander of the Army of the Potomac. General Webb believed the North had finally found the general to lead the army. President Lincoln had been searching for a competent commander ever since the war began. In a letter to his father on July 17, 1863, Webb wrote about his experiences at Gettysburg and his confidence in Meade.

At Gettysburg I fought my Brigade twice and I won their confidence. The Rebels give me credit for pretty good fighting. Since I lost 482 men and 42 (officers) out of a little less than 900 men and 74 officers present with at the assault I think the fight must be considered a severe one. Out of the 482 men only 47 are missing and 20 of those missing I think were taken out of my lines as prisoners.

The Rebels were determined to break though and they actually took from me nearly one third of my fence and wall. Gen. Armistead was mortally wounded after he had passed me. I was a few paces in front of my men, he jumped the wall with about 150 of his men. Himself and 42 men died suddenly. I took six battle flags, more than double my number prisoners. . . . No men ever fought better than my men.

I was just 39 paces from thousand of Rebs. Their officers desired to have me shot and yet they only got one little round on the inside of my right thigh. It is well already. My loss was truly fearful and I was almost disgraced. But all my command knew that we were never to leave that hill or mound. The 69th lost all its field officers but they obeyed orders. After the Rebs were inside the fence I went to them and told them to (not known) to a man they replied that I could count on them.

I have been though many battles, in all sorts of places, under all fires but never have I heard such a cannonading as they opened upon my lines and when they concentrated 110 pieces upon myself and the brigade on my left, it was terrible. The assault was nobly made. It was a magnificent and terrible military (maneuver) and for a while they fairly overwhelmed me. (Colonel Norman) Hall, commanding the brigade on my left, a young West Pointer, helped me at the right time. He sent few men but a good many colors. It looked like strong reinforcements.

Poor Annie (Webb's wife) has a hard time now. It is worse for her than for me. To die in such a fight is nothing, to lose a husband is a terrible thing. But God protected me last time. If I am yet to be one of his instruments in putting down the Rebellion; I will be spared again. I feel firmly that He does protect individuals . . . Rely on Meade. The man we have been looking for, the best we have discovered.

Your ever affectionate Son, Andy.[144]

Webb wrote a letter to his wife Annie on July 27 and expected Gettysburg to be the victory that would ensure the preservation of the Union. "I am now confident of success. . . . I believe 200,000 conscripts will finish this business. I expect to see Jeff Davis a prisoner. . . . You need not expect me to expose myself unnecessarily in any more battles. (At) Gettysburg the fate of a county depended upon individuals. . . . Had Pickett broken though my lines this army would have been (defeated)."[145]

For Union General Meade, he believed Gettysburg was a great victory and wrote so to his wife two days after the fighting concluded. "It was a grand battle and is in my judgment a most decided victory, (though) I did not annihilate or bag the Confederate army. The men behaved splendidly. They endured long marches short rations and stood one of the terrific cannonading I ever witnessed."[146]

President Abraham Lincoln, though thankful that the Rebels had been repulsed at Gettysburg, was vexed at Meade not pursuing and annihilating the Confederate army. Meade would continue guiding the Army of the Potomac but over-all command of Union forces would soon be transferred to another recently victorious Union officer, General Ulysses S. Grant. The day after Pickett's Charge, Grant gained another major Northern victory at Vicksburg, Mississippi. Grant's forces took almost 30,000 prisoners after Confederate General John C. Pemberton surrendered his army. The South lost another 3,000 soldiers on the battlefield. The combination of the victories at Gettysburg and Vicksburg dealt a major blow to the military effectiveness of the South.

Joseph P. Elliot, Quartermaster of the 71st Pennsylvania, wrote in his diary that when Webb was wounded he refused to leave the field. Elliott also detailed other losses in his diary. Elliot reported Baxter lost a limb and Duffy killed. Elliot also discussed the wounding of Generals Hancock and Gibbon. He also feared the wound to O'Kane would be fatal. The brigade numbered 515 men after the fight with Colonel Penn Smith temporarily commanding. Elliot stated without exception Gettysburg was the fiercest battle ever fought.

Lieutenant Frank Haskell, who rallied troops to aid Webb, was also wounded as he wrote he was shot in the thigh but the bullet first his saddle and his skin wasn't broken. Many of the survivors of Pickett's Charge wrote about those who were lost. There were plenty of wounded, dead and dying men to memorialize.

"Lt. George Woodruff was shot thought the body wile maneuvering a section of his guns at Ziegler's Grove, but waved off aid. He died the next day. Both of Hays's brigade commanders were also casualties. Col. Smyth had been wounded during the bombardment and later Col. Eliakim Sherrill shot in the stomach, a wound that proved mortal. One of his men said Sherrill was being 'too brave a man to live.'"[147] Sherrill also may have been trying to prove himself to General Hancock as the two officers had a disagreement over the way Sherrill was commanding his troops.

The view of the dead and dying struck Colonel Richard Penn Smith of the 71st Pennsylvania. He wrote to General Isaac Jones Wistar on July 29, 1863. The letter in the files of the Gettysburg National Military Park, stated, "I never saw so much human blood before." Smith wrote that walking without stepping on the dead and dying was almost impossible and the cries of the wounded men were piercing. "For three days I lived among the dead, dying and wounded. The cries of the last were piteous. We could not comfort, it was a graveyard."[148]

The Confederate losses were substantial, especially the officers participating in Pickett's Charge. Southern generals and colonels fell at Gettysburg in great numbers. In all, the losses of dead wounded and captured topped 6,000 soldiers, almost half of the Confederates taking part in the advance. Union General Winfield Scott Hancock listed the number of casualties in the Army of the Potomac as

more than 4,300 killed, wounded and captured. While the
percentage of casualties on both sides was close, the Union
held their position and were the victors.

Some of the Union wounded survived, including 27-year-
old Major James Duffy of the 69th Pennsylvania, who
commanded the unit after his superior officers became
casualties. Duffy's thigh wound caused him to be trans-
ported to Baltimore for treatment and then returned to
his home in Philadelphia. He resigned from the army in
December. The wound bothered him the rest of his life and
he died six years later, June 16, 1869, from complications
of his Gettysburg injury.

Duffy's commander, Dennis O'Kane slipped into a
coma and died during the early morning hours of July 4.
His burial took place on July 9, 1863, in Philadelphia. The
funeral procession was reportedly led by a brass band and
his pallbearers included 16 Union army officers, among
them, three from the 69th Pennsylvania who had been
wounded at Gettysburg. He was buried in Cathedral
Cemetery in an unmarked grave.

* * *

The surgeons worked through the night to save as many
of the wounded of both armies as they could. Supplies were
strained and medical personnel were physically taxed as
they feverishly performed their lifesaving work. Amputa-
tions were common. One Philadelphia Brigade member,
James Eva of Company K, 106th Pennsylvania, lost his
left arm when the doctors discovered his wrist wound

had caused serious nerve damage. Wounded soldiers were brought into hospitals hours after the last shots were fired. Members of the 71st Pennsylvania used lanterns and candles for lights while searching the field that night for wounded comrades. William J. Burns of the 71st Pennsylvania wrote that on Independence Day 1863 his unit spent the day at the stone wall. Rain fell during the morning and the previous night. Each man, according to Burns, had three loaded muskets. The day after Pickett's Charge proved to be a wet miserable day and night for the members of the regiment. Burns added that it was a blessed day for the country.

After completing their duties for the night, members of the Philadelphia Brigade had a chance to rest. The soldiers had been give rations for three days and for the moment were under command of Colonel Richard Penn Smith of the 71st Pennsylvania. General Alexander Webb had been elevated to division command after the wounding of General John Gibbon. A thunderstorm rolled through Gettysburg and Smith is said to have questioned if the thunderous artillery duel earlier in the day that anything to do with the storm.

Smith and the 71st Pennsylvania fought well at Gettysburg despite Smith's withdrawal at Culp's Hill without orders on the night of July 2, 1863. Generals Webb and Hancock both noted Smith's leadership during the fighting at the Angle.

General George Stannard had high praise for his Vermont regiments. His report in the Official Records of the War of the Rebellion stated, "The members of my staff—Capt. William H. Hill, assistant adjutant-general; Lieuts. George W. Hooker and G. G. Benedict, aides-de-camp; Lieutenant Francis G. Clark, provost-marshal, and Lieut. S. F. Prentiss, ordinance officer—executed all my orders with the utmost promptness, and by their coolness under fire and good example contributed essentially to the success of the day. There were 350 killed, wounded, and missing from my three regiments engaged; of the missing, only 1 is known to have been taken prisoner."[149]

The Official Records of the War of the Rebellion contains reports by many of the Union generals, including John Gibbon. General Gibbon wrote in part:

> The repulse of this assault was most gallant, and I desire to call special attention to the great gallantry and conspicuous qualities displayed by Brigadier-General Webb and Colonel Hall. Their services were invaluable, and it is safe to say that, without their presence, the enemy would have succeeded in gaining a foothold at that point.
>
> Attention is also called to the officers and men specially mentioned by the various reports.
>
> I desire to call particular attention to the manner in which several of the subordinate reports mention the services of my gallant aide, Lieut. F. A. Haskell, Sixth Wisconsin, and to add my testimony of his valuable services. This young officer has been through many battles, and distinguished himself alike in all by his

conspicuous coolness and bravery, and in this one was slightly wounded, but refused to quit the field. It has always been a source of regret to me that our military system offers no plan for rewarding his merit and services as they deserve.

Major Baird, Eighty-second New York, my division inspector-general, received a severe wound in the foot while gallantly carrying an order for me on the 2d. Such men as these should be promoted on the field, though I regret to say they are frequently overlooked by the State authorities, and incompetent persons (not soldiers) placed over their heads. I have urged Major Baird for the colonelcy of his regiment, now vacant.

Captain John P. Wood, assistant adjutant-general, was injured by his horse being shot and falling upon him early on the 3d. Captain Wessels, One hundred and sixth Pennsylvania, my division judge-advocate, and Lieutenant Moale, Nineteenth U. S. Infantry, aide-de-camp, were with me on the field, and behaved with great coolness and gallantry.

Our batteries were served in the most gallant style, continuing their fire to the last under the most trying circumstances. The heavy loss in officers and men, horses and *matériel* attest at the same time the severity of the enemy's fire and the noble manner in which it was sustained.

Our loss in killed and wounded was fearful, especially among the field officers, demonstrating how gallantly the men were led. Colonel Ward, Fifteenth Massachusetts;

Lieutenant-Colonel Huston, Eighty-Second New York;
Colonel O'Kane and Lieutenant-Colonel Tschudy, Sixty-
ninth Pennsylvania; Colonel Revere, Twentieth Massachusetts; Lieutenant-Colonel Steele, Seventh Michigan,
and Lieutenant-Colonel Thoman, Fifty-ninth New York,
were killed; and Colonel Baxter, Seventy-second Pennsylvania; Colonel Colvill, Lieutenant-Colonel Adams,
and Major Downie, First Minnesota: Lieutenant-Colonel
Macy, Twentieth Massachusetts, and Lieutenant-Colonel
Wass and Major Rice, Nineteenth Massachusetts, were
wounded. The division went into action about 3,800
strong; lost in killed and wounded over 1,600, and captured more prisoners than it had men on the ground at
the end of the conflict, besides many colors.[150]

General Hancock's report in the Official Records of
the War of the Rebellion also details many of the acts
of bravery performed by his men. Hancock reported:

For the services of the commanders of divisions,
Brig. Gens. John Gibbon, Alexander Hays, and John
C. Caldwell, I need only to refer to the history of the
deeds of their commands. Brig. Gens. John Gibbon and
Alexander Hays, being more particularly under my eye
in the crisis of the battle, it is but just that I should state
that their conduct was all that could be desired in division commanders.

Capt. J. G. Hazard, commander of artillery of the
corps, performed his duty in a commendable manner,
behaving in the field with gallantry and directing his
artillery with skill and judgment. I desire particularly

to refer to the services of a gallant young officer, First Lieut. F. A. Haskell, aide-de-camp to Brigadier-General Gibbon, who, at a critical period of the battle, when the contending forces were but 50 or 60 yards apart, believing that an example was necessary, and ready to sacrifice his life, rode between the contending lines with the view of giving encouragement to ours and leading it forward, he being at that moment the only mounted officer in a similar position. He was slightly wounded and his horse was shot in several places.

Brigadier-General Webb; Col. N.J. Hall, commanding brigade; Colonel Devereux, Nineteenth Massachusetts; Colonel Mallon, Forty-second New York; Col. R. Penn Smith, Seventy-first Pennsylvania, and others, whom I regret I am unable to name, performed in like manner most distinguished services in leading their men forward at a critical period in the contest.

Captain Hall, Fifty-third Pennsylvania Volunteers, and Lieutenant Taylor, both of the signal corps, are entitled to mention at my hands for their energy and usefulness displayed during the entire battle.[151]

Hancock had additional high praise for Webb. He said, "In every battle and on every important field there is one spot to which every army (officer) would wish to be assigned, the spot upon which centers the fortunes of the field. There was but one such spot at Gettysburg and it fell to the lot of Gen'l Webb to have it and hold it and for holding it he must receive the credit due him."[152]

The reports of the battlefield commanders give credence to the theory that the unsung heroes of Gettysburg were the field officers of the Union army.

Hancock also lamented the loss of good men. "This great victory was not gained without irreparable losses. In addition to those previously mentioned, the following regimental commanders were killed: Col. Dennis O'Kane, Sixty-ninth Pennsylvania Volunteers; Lieut. Col. Max A. Thoman, Fifty-ninth New York Volunteers; Col. Richard P. Roberts, One hundred and fortieth Pennsylvania Volunteers (on the 2d); Col. P. J. Revere, Twentieth Massachusetts Volunteers, and Lieutenant-Colonel Steele, Seventh Michigan Volunteers. The number of casualties among the field officers was very great, many of the regiments losing them all.

"Three of the battery commanders, Captain Rorty and Lieuts. A. H. Cushing and G. A. Woodruff, all able, experienced, and distinguished officers, were killed, and another battery commander, Lieut. T. F. Brown, First Rhode Island Artillery, severely wounded. The losses of the corps during the action at Gettysburg amounted to 4,323 officers and men killed, wounded, and missing. The strength of the corps in the action was about 10,000 officers and men."[153]

As for the commander of the Philadelphia Brigade, General Alexander Webb pointed out the action of Colonel Richard Penn Smith and others in his report. "Colonel Smith, commanding the Seventy-first Pennsylvania Volunteers, threw two companies of his command behind the stone wall on the right of Cushing's battery, 50 paces retired from the point of attack. This disposition of his troops was most important. Colonel Smith showed true military intelligence on the field."

Webb summed up his losses, 43 commissioned officers and more than 500 enlisted men, and wrote, "I lost gallant officers and men. They need no tribute from me. The conduct of this brigade was most satisfactory. Officers and men did their whole duty."

The total casualties, including killed, wounded, missing and captured, for Gettysburg has been stated as 23,230 Confederate and 23,050 Union. Webb's command lost 44 percent of his 940. The 69th Pennsylvania lost 47 percent of its strength during the fighting at the copse of trees.[154] John Busey's *Regimental Strengths & Losses at Gettysburg,* reported Webb lost 491 out of 1,224 officers and men, total loss of 40 percent.

※ ※ ※

Family members of the soldiers lost in battle traveled to Gettysburg to reclaim their bodies. Two of the Steffan brothers, John and Edward, were from Philadelphia and members of the 72nd Pennsylvania. A third brother, August, heard of John's death but didn't have any information on Edward's condition, so August traveled to Gettysburg.

His quest to find information about his brothers is detailed in the files of the Gettysburg National Military Park. August Steffan left Philadelphia for Baltimore on Monday, July 6, 1863, and arrived at 4:30 a.m. where he stayed at the Eutaw House. August didn't go to bed but took breakfast and then managed to obtain a military pass to visit Gettysburg. He traveled that night on the Western Maryland Railroad and made it to the Relay House, just seven miles from the battleground.

August found the roads almost impassible and hired an old rickety wagon. "We hired a team and visited the battlefield—the road five miles from Littlestown is lined with hospitals. We entered nearly all in order to inquire after Ed. & ascertain where poor John had met his death and was buried. Such scenes of horror I never witnessed, in fact I would not have believed it possible, had I not seen for myself—wounded men in every condition—some with arms and legs off—wounds in all parts of the body & no attention paid to them whatever. Moans and groans of anguish struck upon your ear from every side—the 2nd Army Corp. Hospital was decidedly the worst—here were nearly all dangerous wounds & by a great deal the largest number of men.

"In going through the woods we passed one spot where some 30 to 40 bodies in an advanced state of decomposition awaited burial, they had died after being brought to the Hospital. Close by was a trench filled, but not yet covered—further on we met a party of soldiers carrying a wounded comrade—they set him down in order to rest themselves—& while there the unfortunate man breathed his last. Around stood his fellow soldiers laughing and talking, wholly unimpressed by the scene, it is surprising how this bloody & unnatural war brutalizes all the finer feelings of a man—most of the men who have been in service any time seem totally void of any such traits of humanity which are natural & proper in a civilized being.

"We, after some search, found a surgeon attached to John's brigade, who gave us the direction to that part of the field where he was buried with a few other officers. We then proceeded to the battlefield. The sight here was terrible in the extreme—everything indicated that here 200,000 men probably had struggled for existence. The field is strewn with accoutrements & all the equipments appertaining to large armies. Graves cover the ground in every direction. Where the Phila. Brigade stood and fought so bravely, the field gives every indication of a bloody conflict. In the vicinity are numerous graves of the 69, 71, 72 & 106 Penna. Rgts. Which attest the desperation & courage which these noble fellow defended the soil of their native state."[155]

* * *

General Alexander Webb wrote several letters to his wife in the weeks following Gettysburg on his participation in the great battle. "(We) fought on 2nd and 3rd. Lost 428 men and 42 officers of my command. Took six colors, 900 muskets and more prisoners than I had men. Genl. Armistead was killed within 40 feet of me and in my rear. I had a fearful fight received a slight scratch inside my thigh from a Mississippi rifle. But my clothes holy. Horse wounded. We have whipped them everywhere and they ran off. Gone; run; whipped. God be praised. Goodbye. Andy."[156]

His second letter is dated August 1, 1863, and read, "July 4: Cloudy and very warm all day. Wind S. W. in the afternoon a heavy rain fell accompanied by thunder and lightning. A batch of some four thousand prisoners arrived in town today from the front—Rebel General Armistead was brought in by two men of K Company. 71st PV on a stretcher. Our regiment captured two stands of colors from the enemy."[157]

Webb's Official Records of the War of the Rebellion report stated his brigade captured nearly 1,000 prisoners, 6 battle flags and picked up 1,400 stand of arms and 903 sets of accouterments.

Webb's description of his own conduct was modest. He won accolades from his superiors and a Congressional Medal of Honor for his valor at Gettysburg. The medal's citation is also modest and reads, "Distinguished personal gallantry in leading his men forward at a critical period in the contest."[158] The medal was bestowed on Webb on September 28, 1891.

The Congressional Medal of Honor was initiated during he Civil War. On December 9, 1861, Iowa Senator James W. Grimes introduced Senate bill number 82. The medal was originally designed to promote the efficiency of the Navy by authorizing the production and distribution of medals of honor. Within weeks the bill was passed and President Lincoln signed the legislation.

In February 1862 Massachusetts Senator Henry Wilson introduced a similar bill to authorize the President to distribute medals to privates in the Army of the United States who shall distinguish themselves in battle. Wording was changed and on July 12, 1862, the Army Medal of Honor was born.

The first act recognized for a Medal of Honor was for the killing of the murderer of Colonel Ellsworth at the Marshall House Alexandria, Virginia. The medal went to Private Francis Brownell of New York. At Gettysburg 58 Medals of Honor were awarded to Union soldiers, including 30 for service on July 3, 1863. The recipients:

Private Elijah Bacon, 14th Connecticut, captured the 16th North Carolina flag. He was killed the next year at the Battle of the Wilderness.

2nd Lieutenant George Benedict, 12th Vermont, delivered orders under fire.

Captain Morris Brown, 126th New York, captured a flag.

Private John Clopp, 71st Pennsylvania, captured 9th Virginia flag.

Corporal Joseph De Castro, 19th Massachusetts, captured 19th Virginia flag.

Sergeant George Dore, 126th New York, saved unit's colors from enemy.

Sergeant Benjamin Falls, 19th Massachusetts, captured a flag.

Corporal Christopher Flynn, 14th Connecticut, captured 52nd North Carolina flag.

Sergeant Frederick Fuger, Battery A, 4th U. S. Artillery, commanded artillery unit after all officers in his unit had been killed.

Sergeant William Hincks, 14th Connecticut, captured 14th Tennessee flag

Sergeant Benjamin Jellison, 19th Massachusetts, captured 57th Virginia flag and prisoners.

Private John Mayberry, 1st Delaware, captured a flag.

Private Bernard McCarren, 1st Delaware, captured a flag.

Captain John Miller, 8th Ohio, captured two flags

Captain William Miller, 3rd Pennsylvania Calvary, led a charge to stop the enemy.

Corporal Henry O'Brien, 1st Minnesota, saved company colors from the enemy.

Private George Platt, 6th U.S. Calvary, saved colors from the enemy.

Corporal William Raymond, 108th New York, for bringing ammunition to comrades while under fire.

Major Edmund Rice, 19th Massachusetts, for bravery during countercharge against Pickett's forces.

Private James Richmond, 8th Ohio, captured a flag.

Private John Robinson, 19th Massachusetts, captured 57th Virginia flag.

Private Oliver Rood, 20th Indiana, captured 21st North Carolina flag.

Private Martin Schwenk, 6th U. S. Calvary, rescued wounded soldier.

Private Marshall Sherman, 1st Minnesota, captured 28th Virginia flag.

Sergeant James Thompson, 1st Pennsylvania Rifles, captured 15th Georgia flag.

Colonel Wheelock Veazey, 16th Vermont, led a countercharge during Pickett's Charge.

Private Jerry Wall, 126th New York, captured a flag.

General Alexander Webb, distinguished personal gallantry.

Major William Wells, 1ˢᵗ Vermont Cavalry, led a daring charge.

Sergeant James Wiley, 59ᵗʰ New York, captured a Georgia flag.

General Hancock reported on the capture of enemy flags and the heroics of his men in his Official Records of the War of the Rebellion report. "After a few moments of desperate fighting the enemy's troops were repulsed, threw down their arms, and sought safety in flight or by throwing themselves on the ground to escape our fire. The battle-flags were ours and the victory was won.

"Gibbon's division secured 12 (flags) and prisoners enough to swell the number captured by the corps to about 4,500. . . . I desire to bring particularly to the notice of the major-general commanding the case of Sergt. Frederick Fuger, first sergeant of Battery A, Fourth U.S. Artillery. During the action of the 3d, his conduct was such as to entitle him to promotion, and his character is such as to make this a proper method of rewarding his services.

"With reference to the number of colors taken from the enemy, it is proper to say that each division has been credited with the number actually turned in, and for which receipts are held, making the aggregate of twenty-seven. There were undoubtedly thirty-three colors captured, the balance having been secreted as individual trophies."[159]

According to Anthony McDermott of the 69th Pennsylvania, many of the flags were picked up from wounded or killed Confederate color-bearers without any heroics. McDermott did give credit to Private John Clopp of the 71st Pennsylvania. Clopp, according to McDermott, physically took the flag away from the color-bearer of the 9th Virginia.

General Hancock noted Frederick Fuger in his report. Fuger, born in Germany in 1836, came to the United States in 1853 and joined the army three years later. Fuger took over the command of Battery A after the death of Lieutenant Alonzo Cushing. He also engaged in hand-to-hand fighting when the Confederates breeched the stone wall. He served the rest of the war, was promoted to Lieutenant Colonel and died on October 13, 1913.

General Webb wrote about receiving the flag of the 19th Virginia from De Castro. "At the instant a man broke through my lines and thrust a rebel battle flag into my hands. He never said a word and darted back. It was Corporal Joseph H. De Castro, one of my color bearers. He had knocked down a color bearer in the enemy's line with the staff of the Massachusetts State colors, seized the falling flag and dashed it to me."[160]

Medal winner Colonel Veazey went on to become a justice of the Vermont Supreme Court. He was born in Brentwood, New Hampshire, on December 5, 1835, and began practicing law in 1860. His citation reads, "Rapidly assembled his regiment and charged the enemy's flank; charged front under heavy fire, and charged and destroyed a Confederate brigade, all this with new troops in their first battle."

The great number of prisoners also caused issues for the victors. A member of the 71st Pennsylvania reported seeing captured Southerners picking up supplies off the field and was concerned weapons would also be gathered. Indeed, officers at Fort Delaware, where many Rebels captured at Gettysburg were taken, reported knives in prisoners' possession.

Some of the members of the 69th Pennsylvania captured by the Rebels died in Confederate prisons, according to an accounting in the Bachelder Papers in the Gettysburg National Military Park files. The report stated George Mulholland of Company F died at Camp Parole on November 19, 1863; James O'Neill of Company F died at Andersonville, Georgia, on June 13, 1864; Henry Thomas of Company F died at Annapolis, Maryland, on July 11, 1863; Arthur Mulholland of Company F died at Richmond, Virginia, date unknown; John McKenny of Company F died at Richmond, Virginia, on November 20, 1863; Patrick Rafferty of Company F died at Richmond, Virginia, on October 15, 1863; Arthur McLaughlin of Company F died at Richmond, Virginia, on February 7, 1864; and Andrew Gallagher of Company G died at Richmond, Virginia, date unknown.

* * *

The survivors of the Philadelphia Brigade celebrated the heroics of their colleagues and mourned losses of dear friends while being thankful for being spared during Pickett's Charge. What took place on July 3, 1863, was difficult to forget. Captain George Meade wrote in a letter in 1882 that he had visited Gettysburg in 1881 and "went over the whole field, and everything came back to me as if it had only just occurred."[161]

The spirit and courage of Lieutenant Anthony McDermott of the 69th Pennsylvania was typical. He reported being a young private of Company at the time of the battle. He then became a company clerk and had his rifle taken from him so he couldn't participate in the battle. McDermott wrote to Colonel John Bachelder on June 2, 1886. "His object was that if the Adjt. and his clerk were both disabled it would be a difficult matter to transact the business of the rgt. properly for some time afterwards. I always disregarded these instructions and at Gettysburg I filled my pockets with cartridges, and before noon on the 2d I got a rifle from a wounded picket and endeavored to discharge my duty as a soldier, and as an American. I was then in my nineteenth year."[162]

A member of the 106th Pennsylvania, John Wheaton Lynch, summed up the feeling of many of the survivors of Gettysburg when he wrote to Bessie Mustin of Philadelphia on July 5, 1863. "With what gratitude I feel towards Almighty God for his marvelous protecting care which he has shown towards me in this late engagement none can tell. O, it seems all most incredible after going through with what I have in the last two days that I am yet spared—not a scratch excepting the left side of my face which is well spattered with powder, making quite a number of spots—we have lost very heavily."[163]

Chapter 9

THE TRIAL

THE REPULSE OF the last Rebel from the Angle, the gathering of the broken and discarded haversacks, knives, rifles and other equipment and the burial of the last casualty did not conclude the battle at Gettysburg.

As years passed, monuments were erected on the hallowed ground of Gettysburg, as President Lincoln pronounced the battlefield in his Gettysburg Address of 1863. Gettysburg was transformed into fields of monuments. While touring the battlefield, today's visitors will find them along the roads and in the fields, almost everywhere they look.

In 1864, a year after the battle, the first steps were taken in the organization of what has become today's national park. The Gettysburg Battlefield Memorial Association was created with a $6,000 grant from the Commonwealth of Pennsylvania. Land was acquired along the defensive positions of the Union army at Gettysburg. Monuments began to be erected in the 1870's.

One special place of honor for the erection of a monument was along the stone wall at the Angle.

Fittingly, the original sites selected for the monuments of the 69th Pennsylvania and the 71st Pennsylvania regiments of the Philadelphia Brigade were within the Angle near the stone wall. The original spot selected for the placement of the 72nd Pennsylvania monument was northeast east of the copse of trees on the ridge where the unit soldiers stood firm and helped repulse Pickett's Charge.

The Gettysburg Battlefield Memorial Association, the organization in charge of selecting locations for the erection of the monuments, directed the 72nd Pennsylvania monument "should be placed 283 feet in the rear of the stone fence at the Bloody Angle."[164]

The survivors of the 72nd Pennsylvania were offended by the placement; they wanted a place of honor next to the monuments of the 71st Pennsylvania and 69th Pennsylvania at the stone wall. In fact, the survivors wanted their monument erected mid-way between the monuments of the 69th Pennsylvania and 71st Pennsylvania regiments.

The Pennsylvania State Monument Commission was contacted and after the veterans were heard the commissioners approved a location twenty feet behind the stone wall if the location was within the rules of the Gettysburg Battlefield Memorial Association. In December 1888 Philadelphia Brigade veteran John Reed began digging a foundation for a monument without the battlefield association's approval. Reed was arrested and a lawsuit began. A three-year court battle took place before judges of both the Adams County and the Pennsylvania Supreme Court.

The 72nd Pennsylvania contended during the fight at the "Bloody Angle" members of the unit "during the charge of the enemy, it rushed down into the Bloody Angle and drove back the enemy, in mass, into the angle, and there fought them hand to hand so desperately that it ended in the death or capture of every one of the enemy, that had crossed the stone fence."

The named plaintiffs were John Reed, Sylvester Byrne, Frederick Middleton, Julius D. Allen and Charles W. Devitt, representing the survivors. The suit was filed in Adams County Court on January 7, 1889. Adams County Court agreed with a contention of the Gettysburg Battlefield Memorial Association to dismiss the case but the 72nd Pennsylvania survivors appealed the ruling to the Supreme Court on March 23, 1889, and the court overturned the lower court's ruling and sent the case back to Adams County for another hearing.

Testimony was given by the survivors a quarter century after the struggle. After such a period memories of individuals can become fuzzy and, for sure, some of the testimony by witnesses was slanted as to give credence to the placement of the 72nd Pennsylvania monument at the wall, but individual recollections of moments of combat during Pickett's Charge adds to the rich recorded history of Gettysburg.

The court records begin with the history of the case. To set the scene, the court record reported:

The 69th, 71st, 72nd and 106th regiments of Pennsylvania volunteers composed the 'Philadelphia Brigade,' commanded by Brigadier General Alexander S. Webb. About 1 p.m. the terrific cannonading began, the objective point being the left center of the Union forces. At this point was a clump of trees, and in front of it a stone wall extending north and south about 150 yards in length, and at the north end an angle formed by a stone wall running back east about two hundred feet, and then running north again. There was a rise of ground from the front stone wall as it neared the northeast corner, back south to the crest of the hill about 250 feet, and making an elevation of about five feet.

Cannonading began. 69th was along the stone wall in front of the clump of trees, and two companies of the 71st at the angle and the other eight companies of the regiment in the rear to the left along the stone wall extending north from the rear. On the crest of the hill in the rear was the 4th U.S. Artillery. Cushing received fire and all but two or three guns disabled. One was taken to the stone wall.[165]

The crux of the defense case was the 72nd Pennsylvania was the second line of the Philadelphia Brigade as the fighting began on the afternoon of July 3, 1863. The unit was "in the rear of the trees, and advanced to a position about 300 feet in the rear of the stone wall behind the crest of the hill when the enemy advanced." The 72nd Pennsylvania fired from that position and General Webb failed to get the 72nd Pennsylvania to advance to assist the 69th and 71st Pennsylvania units. The defense claimed at no time did the 72nd Pennsylvania advance to drive back Pickett's forces.

To bolster its contention, the defense quoted the Official Records of the War of the Rebellion. "General Webb in his official report of July 12, 1863, when the facts of that fight were fresh in memory and honestly reported, says, 'The Seventy-second regiment fought steadily and persistently, but the enemy would probably have succeeded in piercing our lines, had not Colonel Hall advanced with several of his regiments to my support, defeated, routed, the enemy, fled in disorder.'"[166]

The Bachelder papers at Gettysburg National Military Park contain a letter written by Lieutenant Anthony W. McDermott, former adjutant of the 69th Pennsylvania to Colonel John B. Bachelder. The letter of October 21, 1889, contends the 72nd Pennsylvania was not at the wall.

"I am much rejoiced at your determination to thoroughly investigate as to who repulsed Pickett's charge and what troops took part therein," McDermott wrote. "When the strict truth of the details of that affair come out you will know that I have not claimed too much for my regiment. The 69th has never claimed that no other troops came to their assistance for we always allow that Hall's brigade came up and were followed by the 72nd, also that the 71st Penna. Added on our right, and the 59th N.Y., 19th Maine, 15th, 20th and 19th Mass, 42nd, 20th and 82nd New York, 1st Minn., 7th Mich. and Stannard's brigade all aided on our left in repulsing Pickett, but we claim that no troops came to the wall at our position either before or after the battle. Not one of the 11 regiments you mention came to the wall as such at any time, notwithstanding their official reports says so. Hall's brigade came no further to our right than the clump of trees."[167]

McDermott also wrote that the capture of Confederate

battle flags did not prove any unit was at the wall as all flags were taken after the Southerners were defeated.

In an earlier letter, September 17, 1889, McDermott wrote to Bachelder that the 72nd Pennsylvania didn't come to the wall until Webb shouted "Yes boys, the enemy is running, come up, come up!"

Bachelder replied to McDermott's letter on September 27, 1889, and McDermott had words of caution for Bachelder. "You will have to be very careful or the 72nd Regt people will best you, McDermott wrote. "They seem to be working the idea that your commission is making the point that it was the 19th Mass. And the 42nd N.Y. who fought in the 'Angle' and not the 72nd Pa." In the letter, McDermott gave a list of 23 names of former soldiers who would testify that the 72nd Pennsylvania did not fight at the wall. Also, McDermott questioned the testimony given by "Jon Buckley" of Company K of his old unit in favor of the 72nd Pennsylvania. "I cannot understand how he could give any testimony for or against the 72nd ... Buckley told me, about two years ago, that the men on the left of the regt. Were crouched behind the wall on one or both knees and that some of Pickett's men actually stepped over them. This being the case and amid the excitement and smoke of battle, the obstructed view along his right of 8 companies, how could he tell what was going on so far to his right."[168]

At the time McDermott wrote to Bachelder:

The rest of the brief history of Pickett's Charge the court record included continued:

By the few artillerists that were left, and the other gun was run down and manned in the angle by the men of the Seventy-first regiment. About this time the infantry of the enemy commenced to advance a half mile distant, and moved en echelon and struck the stone wall near the angle. The Seventy-second regiment had been placed in reserve behind the copse of trees and in the protection of the crest of the hill, in support of the battery, and at this juncture they were hurriedly brought up to crest of the hill by an oblique movement and halted, with the right resting on the north, stone wall, near the rear angle, and the left extending nearly on a line with the rear of the copse of trees and distant about two hundred feet from the front stone wall in the Bloody Angle, thus covering the space which had been occupied by Cushing's battery. There they were drawn up in line of battle and received the fire of the enemy, who had now reached the stone wall and were pouring over it into the angle in great numbers. The regiment fired upon them for a few moments, the enemy to the number of about one hundred and fifty men, occupying the angle and moving more than half way up from the angle to the Seventy-second. Two companies of the Sixty-ninth regiment were thrown back at right angles to the stone wall, and fired into the enemy in the angle. The two companies of the Seventy-first were driven back, or taken prisoners. The remaining companies of the Seventy-first at the stone wall in the rear, and extending north, fired into the angle upon the enemy. Other regiments of Hall's brigade came up along and through the copse of trees and fired in the angle. There was there transverse firing upon the enemy from three sides. General Armistead, the intrepid leader, fell mortally wounded about midway between the Seventy-second regiment and the stone wall, where he fell the enemy threw down their guns, threw up their hands and surrendered, and the adjutant of the brigade, Colonel Banes, caused the Seventy-second regiment, still in line on the crest of the hill, to open ranks and pass the prisoners through to the rear. The battle was ended.[169]

For the plaintiffs, a number of surviving members of the 72nd Pennsylvania testified about the moments they claimed they fought the remnants of Lee's division at the Angle. All of the testimony supported the contention that the unit took part of the fight at the stone wall at the crucial time when the outcome of Pickett's Charge was still in doubt.

One of the stories in support of the placement of the 72nd Pennsylvania monument at the wall came from Private William H. Good of the unit. He testified that when they started down on the front and they ran within about 16 or 18 feet of the stone wall, and came into it pretty sharp there; company E and K advanced over the stone wall. The regiment flag was with them, he testified, at the wall and when they went over the wall. Good also stated that night he was detailed to bury the dead and found his chum who had fallen crossways across the stone wall. He stated some of the dead of his unit were found at the wall itself.

Good, who was employed by the Federal Mint in Philadelphia at the time of the trial, testified about General Webb's efforts to get the unit to advance. "General Webb made a whole lot of motions, or sword motions, and we advanced. That would be towards the 71st and then as soon as we advanced along to the 71st he commenced to pull his sword this way. He might have said something but it would very hard for anybody to hear what he did say. He might have said a great many things, but I can't tell what he said. It was all done with motions.

"Then we started down on the front and we ran within about sixteen or eighteen feet I think of the stone wall and we came into it pretty sharp here. Company E and K advanced over the stone wall. On the other side of the stone wall from us, when we advanced over, we found a lot of blue rocks running on a pitch slanting that way. When we jumped over that some of us slid down quick. I did myself. It got so warm on that side of the stone fence that some were shooting this way and some were shooting the other, and it got to be a regular jumble. It was a rough and tumble fight after the firing chiefly ceased, in line — after we charged over the stone wall."[170]

Good said he lost sight of General Webb. "I don't know where he went to. Of course, you don't know hardly where people go. In fact, in a place like that you don't watch for what people do. We had all we could do in here and it would be impossible to tell where a man went and what he did. Anybody who has been in an action knows you could not explain that point because you have got all you can possibly do to get down to work."[171]

According to Private James Wilson of the 72nd Pennsylvania, his unit did obey the orders of General Webb to advance to the stone wall. "When I was about ten feet from the wall I was wounded. After I was wounded the regiment went to the wall; on the way to the wall we were advancing and firing and they were advancing and firing; this was kept up until we came hand-to-hand in some instances; we had quite a little dispute, before we came to the stone wall; we fought hand-to-hand and clubbed guns."[172]

Lieutenant Henry Russell of Company A of the 72nd Pennsylvania, who was a manufacturer of artists' material after the war, also testified about Webb's efforts to lead his unit to the stone wall. He testified, "Company A covered part of the woods when we were firing, General Webb was near to me at the time, and I told General Webb that I couldn't fire because there were men in front of me. I was afraid of hurting them, and he gave a command by the right flank but it couldn't be heard, I had to go and force the men up past this clump of trees, so they could fire.

"We were firing and fighting and General Webb gave the command to charge bayonets. It couldn't be heard, I don't suppose from ten feet away. I heard it distinctly, and was the first one to give this command to my company to fix bayonets. They did fix bayonets, and the balance of the regiment took it up. We charged down to the enemy that were down over this wall, and drove them over that wall and captured them, and I went directly to that wall."[173]

Another member of the 72nd Pennsylvania, Private Elwood N. Hamilton, a painter in private life, testified about General Webb rallying members of the Philadelphia Brigade. Hamilton testified, "The battery was to the right. An artilleryman ran away from this battery and came in this direction, and he runs towards General Webb. General Webb drove him back and took his sword and kind of jabbed at the man. The man says, 'There is no use of my going back, all the men are gone, killed.' But however, the man went back."[174]

Private Jesse W. Mews of the 72nd Pennsylvania remembered advancing and fighting all the way to the stone wall. Mews recalled being within five feet of the wall. Mews testified le lived at 1204 Deacon Street., Philadelphia, and worked as an oiler in the city's water department. "We received fire almost immediately when we got to the top of the hill. I suppose the action lasted probably in that line for two or three minutes. Then we commenced to advance, and advanced fighting from there to the stone wall. I was engaged in what was directly in front of me." [175]

A Philadelphia druggist, Private George Hansell of the 72nd Pennsylvania, recalled he was on a skirmish line and when "driven in by Pickett's men, fell in with the Sixty-ninth regiment at the stone wall and went out along the line and joined his regiment. They had all got down to the fence before I got to them; about ten feet from the fence. Hansell said his regiment was "busy fighting" and he was wounded about ten feet from the wall. He said he crawled on his hands and knees. "I thought that if I were to get wounded or killed I wanted to be near somebody who knew me."[176]

Another member of the 72nd Pennsylvania, Private

Thomas Reed, said his unit made a "mad dash" for the stone wall and engaged the Rebels. "I looked down, our regiment was within ten or fifteen yards of the wall and we advanced over the wall," Reed testified. "Our color bearer carried the flag down past the stone wall for some hundred feet or more. He went that far out in front of the wall and we went out after him. . . . We had to fight our way down to get possession of that wall; we captured most of the enemy at the wall."[177]

Private William H. Porter of the 72nd Pennsylvania stated, "We got up and fired, shot and charged to the wall. I was twenty to twenty five feet away when I was wounded in the abdomen." Private Frank Weible, who became a Philadelphia policeman and lived at 425 Fairmont Avenue, added, "After we fired a volley (from behind the battery) we charged right from that position over the stone wall. I went clear to the stone wall."[178]

Private Charles B. Vessels of the 72nd Pennsylvania was adamant that his unit fought at the wall. He testified, "We fought our way down to the stone wall, took some prisoners on way to wall. The rest of the enemy we fought to the wall."[179]

The plaintiffs received support for their position from Robert T. Whittick, color guard of the 69th Pennsylvania, who said the 72nd came to his unit. Whittick, who lived at 158 North Second Street, Philadelphia, and was employed by the E. Stanley Hart printing company, testified, "They mobbed in with us and got right to the wall. I am positive the 72nd regiment was up to the stone wall for I was conversing with some of them."[180]

Second Lieutenant Henry Russell of the 72nd Pennsylvania recalled giving the order to fix bayonets and charging to the wall. Private Edward N. Hamilton of the 72nd Pennsylvania recalled fighting at the wall and being next to the unit's flag. Private George Kames of the 72nd Pennsylvania recalls charging through an opening at the wall and being shot as he advanced ten feet into the field. Kames said a "great many" of his company fought beyond the wall.

Captain Robert McBride of the 72nd Pennsylvania had a vivid recollection of being at the wall. "We charged right down to the wall through the battery; we charged right to the wall, and right there I captured the colors of a rebel standard and drove him to the rear, that was right at the wall and we fought our way down to the wall. I saw some of my men fall there; I had one of the men on my company fall there with the colors; he was killed not less than ten feet from the wall. A good many of the dead of the regiment piled up at the wall. The engagement in the Bloody Angle was a fight, a bloody one."[181]

Medal of Honor winner Frederick Fuger of Battery A, 4th U. S. Artillery testified he saw members of the 72nd Pennsylvania come "right close to the stone wall, where they commenced firing and moving towards the stone wall."

Two officers of the 72nd Pennsylvania also gave evidence supporting the advance to the wall by their unit. Major Samuel Roberts testified, "The color bearer, seizing the stump of the staff of the colors, whirling his hat around his head, moved with the regiment down to the wall, many of our men being wounded or killed in the advance. I advanced down to the wall, a distance of about sixty yards."[182] Colonel Theodore Hesser wrote in his official report the regiment was ordered to advance upon the stone wall to their immediate front and succeeded in routing the enemy and occupying the wall.

Roberts expanded on the issue of the color bearer in a letter to General Webb that is contained in the Bachelder Papers in the Gettysburg National Military Park files. "The color guard was composed of Sergt. (William) Finecy, Corporals Brown, (John) Steptoe, (Charles) Giberson, (Francis) O'Donnell, Kauffman, Willis and (Thomas) Murphy—Sergt. Finecy fell with a half dozen balls in him, all the guard with the exception of Murphy, were killed or wounded, after the color staff had been severed a few inches below where the colors are attached. Murphy seized the remaining portion, and waving his cap advanced the colors to the fence; I was in Command of the regt. Shortly afterward and promoted Murphy Sergt. He was shot through the breast at Spotsylvania and died about six month since. . . . I recollect passing you, at the time you had a man by the collar who had run back from the battery, we passed so rapidly I could not catch fully the import of your remarks or his answer, beyond there were no men to work the battery."[183]

During testimony, some of the soldiers described the mortal wounding of Confederate General Lewis Armistead. One member of Company F of the 72nd Pennsylvania, James Wilson, testified Major Samuel Roberts ordered his men to concentrate fire on Armistead. Wilson testified, "I didn't leave the field after I was wounded (in the left leg). I saw Armistead cross the wall, my attention was called to him by Major Samuel B. Roberts of my regiment who ordered me to fire on him. All he said was 'shoot that man.' Armistead was conspicuous, a general officer. I didn't see where Armistead fell. He was very much alive when I fired at him, yes I fired at him."[184]

Major Roberts, who lived in Germantown and worked as an accountant at the time of the trial, gave an account of his experiences during Pickett's Charge. He testified:

> We were on the second line; I was on the right flank that day, my position was on the left of the regiment. After the cannonading ceased, the regiment got orders to move; we moved by right flank, left oblique; I thought our objective point was the north stone wall. When it reached that point, some twenty to thirty feet below that north angle, Gen. Webb or Col. Hesser, who were on the extreme left, gave the order, 'Front.' I cannot tell which. The right company had moved beyond the regiment, leaving a gap between the companies and that company; I dressed the right company back upon the regiment. As we moved by right flank, I passed General Webb who had a man by the collar, with his sword raised and said to him, 'Where are you going?' The man replied, 'All the men have left the battery.'
>
> We took the fire of the enemy and at that time I judged that not less than eighty of our men fell, firing

commenced then at will. (The enemy) advanced over the stone wall and fell back. The enemy used the stone wall as a barricade. The enemy could neither advance nor retreat and about the center of that wall they (the enemy) placed their colors. All of our color bearers, except one, had been disabled.

For the purpose of dislodging those men behind the wall, the orders were given to advance. I can't tell whether it was Gen. Webb or Col. Hesser as it was on our extreme left. The color bearer, seizing the stump of the staff of the colors, whirling his hat around his head, moved with the regiment down to the wall. Many of our men were wounded or killed in the advance. The men behind that wall, besides the men out in the field, surrendered. The men in the field throwing up their hands and shouting 'don't shoot.' After we had formed the line to the right of the 69th, Lt. Col. Hesser was placed in command of both regiments, the sixty-ninth having lost all their field officers.

Wilcox's division of the Confederates was off to our left and front and were still in line. I advanced with the regiment and went down to the wall, a distance of about 60 yards. The regiment had closed up as well as they could under that the tremendous fire and went down as a body. The regiment simply advanced down receiving the fire of the enemy. It was such a tremendous racket that you couldn't tell who was shooting. I think there was no firing at the wall. There may have been some individual firing.

General Webb made a detail of 45 men under Capt. Whittaker and placed them in the rear of the brigade with orders to shoot at any man that passed a line.[185]

Wilson testified the 72nd Pennsylvania continued to the wall but not in a straight line. "We met with a few of the enemy on the way to the wall; they were captured. We ordered them to throw down their guns and go to the rear; we didn't take them to the rear. We came hand-to-hand in some instances. We had quite a little dispute."[186] He said the men used guns as clubs. "Each man picked out his man. That lasted a very short time and they fell back, what was left of them."[187] Wilson said he also saw one of his officers cut off the head of a Confederate color bearer during the action.

Private Thomas Reed of the 72nd Pennsylvania remembered making a dash for the wall. "On the way down I had occasion to help a stranger; I suppose he was a member of the 69th; he was about to bayonet a rebel that didn't have any arms, and I stopped a moment and stopped him from doing that, and when I looked down our regiment was at the wall. This was within ten or fifteen yards of it."[188]

Individual stories related in the court case did describe some of the horrors suffered by the men of the Philadelphia Brigade. Frederick Mannes, who lived at 2021 North Fifth Street, Philadelphia, was in the flour and feed business and also served as a member of the 19th District School Board. At Gettysburg, Mannes was a sergeant and a member of the color guard of Company B. He said the only fired one shot during the war and the discharge came at Gettysburg.

"After the artillery fire was over the rebels was right on top of us," Mannes testified. "Of course their batteries kept shelling as long as it didn't interfere with their men, but previous to that we moved from the left of the clump of trees to the right with our left resting on the clump of trees. (We) moved by the right flank. Wills was killed and O'Donnell was wounded.

"When Pickett's division came over the wall the regiment rose up and fired. We had been lying down up to that. We raised up and fired, and advanced onto them. We had no bayonets fixed at the time. We advanced towards the rebels, and we hadn't got I don't suppose ten feet from the time we started from near this woods, down towards the wall when I was hit through the ankle. After that I got behind a rock. I tied my leg up. It was bleeding very freely. I kept watching the regiment and seen them going down towards the wall. I hadn't been lying there more than a few minutes when the prisoners begun to come back. There was so many lying dead in this angle here of our men.

"I saw the Rebs stooping down. I suppose there was between five and eight hundred Rebs. They were stooping down and they were picking up haversacks and canteens and blankets, I suppose in captivity to use those things. We having no second line at all, not a man, I thought possibly they might see our weak position and pick up the muskets of the dead men and attack us in the rear. They could have done with one or two men with their wits about them. I called Colonel Baynes' attention to it then, the acting adjutant general of the brigade. . . . A lieutenant colonel of Pickett's division asked me—he saw down the hill that there was nobody behind us at all, and he says, 'Sergeant, where's your reserves?' He had two stars on his collar. 'I told him We can lick you with one line these days, colonel.'"[189]

Captain Robert McBride of Company F recalled seeing members of his unit die at the stone wall and his capturing an enemy flag. McBride, a master warden at the Philadelphia House of Corrections, stated, "The enemy was coming over the wall. They were inside the wall then we commence our fire. We fired some time there and when we charged right to the wall. I captured the colors of a rebel standard and drove him to the rear; that was right at the wall. I took them from him; grabbed them out of his hands. I think it was the 56th Virginia stand of colors I captured. I put my name on it and sent it to brigade headquarters.

"We fought our way down to the wall. I saw some of my men fall there. I had one of the men of my company fall there with the colors, his name was William H. Borman. He was killed not less than ten feet from the wall. He was picked up by one of the men of my company. A number of my men were killed there. We went down and in a straight line, but we fought down to the wall, saw other members of regiment down at the wall, plenty of them. I saw a good many of the dead of the regiment piled up at the wall. They were piled up inside the wall close to the wall."[190]

McBride said he saw General Webb there within a few feet of the stone wall. McBride had a conversation with Webb after the conclusion of Pickett's Charge. McBride recalled that his regiment remained at the stone wall during the night.

The testimony of one member of the 72nd Pennsylvania indicated the unit didn't advance until after the Rebels were repulsed and then they captured prisoners. Corporal Rene Boener, a shoemaker, testified, "After the cannonading ceased we were ordered to get up and prepare for action. And then we were ordered to the right flank. We advanced and stopped there until the enemy had commenced coming over the stone wall."[191]

General Webb testified during the trial and placed the 69th Pennsylvania and 71st Pennsylvania in front and the 72nd Pennsylvania behind the two units behind the copse of trees. "I don't remember the exact distance, but to the best of my recollection it was under cover of the crest of the hill. . . . There was one regiment in reserve to cover up the space the battery held in case it should be destroyed and this was the Seventy-second regiment."[192]

Webb testified about his efforts to have the 72nd Pennsylvania advance to the wall. "I went to their front and center and gave an order for them to move down, but not their commanding officers. They failed to move with me at that time and I passed to the left, to the right of the 69th regiment, to prevent that regiment from being forced back into the clump of trees, if possible. From that point, I saw that the enemy had in some numbers crossed the wall and required the right of the 69th regiment to break and fall to their right and rear and fire upon these troops. At this time, Hall, who was on my left, had, during these few minutes, advanced his regiments in reserve, I hear, to assist our line. . . . The general melee or push took place at this moment and from the raising of their hands on the part of the rebels and dropping of their hands I saw that the charge had failed and the field was ours. I suppose the 72nd regiment during this melee or push was with the whole crowd, the 72nd regiment had first fired from the crest of what I would call a little in advance of the crest. They were in the most exposed position. They had remained in that exposed condition because they had not gone down to the wall.

"The color bearer and myself stood together, I holding on to the staff and he did not move forward with me. I ordered him forward, this was the color bearer of the 72nd regiment. I know of no words said when I ordered him forward, he moved in his place but did not carry the colors out of the regimental line. My adjutant at that time, now Col. Charles H. Banes, I cannot now recall whether I urged him to have the 72nd go forward. The position of the 72nd in line of battle was from the 71st regiment to near the copse of trees, about 50 to 160 feet from the stone wall, maybe more."[193]

Don Ernsberger's book *At The Wall: The 69th Pennsylvania Irish Volunteers at Gettysburg* identifies Sergeant William Finecy as the color bearer that struggled with General Webb. "For a moment a tug of war ensued between the two men, Sergeant Finecy ignoring the Brigadier Generals uniform and stripes."[194]

* * *

188 • PICKETT'S CHARGE: THE UNTOLD STORY

As disputes concerning monuments, including one
involving Pickett's Division, raged, Colonel Richard Penn
Smith of the 71ˢᵗ Pennsylvania, spent some time in Philadelphia in 1887 and was interviewed at the old Lafayette
Hotel by a reporter for the *Philadelphia Times*. An article
from the interview was printed in the *Gettysburg Compiler*
on June 7, 1887. A transcript is contained in the files of the
Gettysburg National Military Park. Smith began by saying
that he would welcome a chance to meet with members of
Pickett's Division at Gettysburg and indeed a number of
reunions did take place.

Smith recalled details of the afternoon of July 3, 1863,
saying, "The enemy opened a most cruel and unceasing
cannonading on the position occupied by the Philadelphia
Brigade . . . the air appeared to be thick with cannon balls,
and the destruction caused by them was the most severe I
had ever seen; the bursting of shell and the havoc and death
made by solid shot and Whitworth bolts made frightful
decimation in the ranks of the Philadelphia Brigade.

"I called for volunteers from my unit (to service the artillery pieces) and the following are the names of those who
promptly responded: Edward F. McMahon, now an officer,
I believe, in the Philadelphia Fire Department; Isaiah Sapp,
who has two medals from the United States Government for
bravery; George Donnelly, Samuel Clawson, John Barlow,
William Brown, George H. Elmer, Corporal John Heap,
Paul Dubin, Albert G. Bunn, Joshua Lainhoff, Peter Ror-
dreuff, James Brown, Margerum and Charles Olcott. "[195]
Smith said the stone wall couldn't protect General Webb's

men. "I immediately flanked to the right and rear and placed them in echelon position behind a rude stone wall, which yielded partial protection from musketry, but a terrible position in which to be torn to pieces by artillery, as that position and a long stretch of front to our right was entirely unprotected. . . . Seeing the vast number of Confederates advancing on us and knowing what a handful of men we had for resistance I directed officers and men to take from a pile of muskets, collected by my regiment on the previous day, as many capped or loaded guns as they could carry, and the officers and men of that position of the regiment went into position behind the stone wall with from three to a dozen loaded guns. I then returned to the left wing of the regiment and ordered Colonel Kochersperger to withhold his fire until the enemy had crossed the Emmitsburg Road, and then to fire and load as rapidly as possible, and when they had been pushed too hard to have time to reload, to fall back substantially on a line with the right of the regiment, and to caution his men on retiring to look out for an enfilading fire from the right of the regiment."[196]

When the Rebels crossed the Emmitsburg Road they marched left towards the 71st Pennsylvania, according to Smith. "The firing became general and the sharp ring of musketry and roar of cannon and thunder of bursting shells made such a deafening noise that the human voice was drowned in the din. . . . The conflict had now become a terrible one. Dead and dying Confederates literally covered the field, mowed down by the many guns in the hands of our men behind the stone wall, which was their only protection from annihilation. Still Pickett's Division marched forward like a solid phalanx on dress parade; neither shot nor shell checked them."[197]

Smith then described the heroics of General Lewis Armistead. "With a dash forward, General Armistead leaped over (the stone wall) followed by his command, crossing the wall in front of the left wing of the 71st. General Armistead, with sword in hand, bravely cheered his men on and the blue and the gray became commingled in a disorganized mass." Smith said the pressure of the Confederates caused his advanced units on the left to retreat and the men fell back to the right wing of the regiment. "At this moment the advancing Virginians met the enfilading fire of the right wing of the 71st. That fire on the enemy was their surprise; it staggered and checked their advance. Armistead was pierced by a ball and fell."[198]

Richard Penn Smith contended the Union center almost cracked under the Confederate pressure. "I do not see how it could have successfully resisted such overwhelming numbers very much longer, and I think had it not been for the great work of the 71st and the 14th Connecticut, and the timely assistance rendered by Stannard's Vermont and Hall's Brigade the Philadelphia Brigade would have no survivors."[199] He said at no time did the Confederate soldiers actually break through the Union line.

* * *

As expected, the conflicting testimony of the military men caused hard feelings and rancor. There were calls for changes in the official reports on Gettysburg filed by Union officers, including General Webb. General Webb stood firm and wouldn't change his report as evidenced by a letter dated June 16, 1888.

Webb wrote, "Yes! Let us have peace. I never have had cause to change my report on Gettysburg. . . . I thought it was all settled this month. . . . Men pressed to the fence after the Rebels laid down their arms, and lots of warriors developed like sand flies when the bullets stopped 'bee-ing' all around our ears."[200]

Despite obvious flaws in the testimony of surviving members of the 72nd Pennsylvania, the Adams County Court eventually ruled in favor of the 72nd Pennsylvania and the decision was upheld by the Pennsylvania Supreme Court. The monument was erected at the unit's desired location at the stone wall.

A letter written on December 10, 1890, by Colonel Arthur F. Devereux of the 19th Massachusetts to the Battlefield Memorial Association is contained in the Bachelder papers at Gettysburg and shows the passion of the Gettysburg veterans. "I see by one of the papers here that the 72nd Pa. won their case against the Battlefield Memorial Association. No details were given. How is it? And if as stated on what grounds? . . . Would your Honorable Board of Trustees permit me to put the monument of my regt. To the front where it belongs or must it stay away back where it gives no sort of idea of the service performed by it? What is the value of a Monument on the field anyhow, when it attempts to enforce a lie? I permitted the removal of my regt's monument back to meet the ideas of the Trustees but not anticipating such a travesty of truth thereby."[201]

At the dedication of the monument on July 4, 1891, plaintiff John Reed, who was arrested for digging a foundation at the beginning of the controversy, said, "Comrades, in your struggle in this angle on July 3, 1863, the God of battles was with you, in your legal contest the Goddess of justice smiled upon you."[202]

Chapter 10

TRUE AMERICAN HERO

A S THE DISTANCE in years grew from the Battle of Gettysburg and Pickett's Charge, the veterans of both armies remembered and relived the events at the Civil War's pivotal battle. Certainly, experts have been analyzing, lauding and criticizing the tactics utilized by those in command at Gettysburg.

General Alexander Stewart Webb was no different from those in his command. Webb's actions at Gettysburg, as has been acknowledged by many and evidenced by being awarded the Medal of Honor, was his most memorable military service. He authored a book published in 1881, *The Peninsula: McClellan's Campaign of 1862*.

A letter Webb wrote to Peter F. Rothermel, who lived at 2020 Race Street, Philadelphia, gave insights to Webb's feelings about Pickett's Charge, the credit due Colonel Norman J. Hall and the incident with the flag bearer of the 72nd Pennsylvania. The letter is contained in the Gettysburg National Military Park files but the date, other than it was written in January and while Webb was at West Point, is unreadable.

The letter stated, "Col. Hall deserves more credit than he gets. Do be prepared to give it to him. The (sergeant) of the 72nd I believe did not live after I took hold of his colors. He pulled back and did not go to the front. I could not drag him forward. So let it be. Rather let him be forgotten. The moment of hesitation of the enemy is the moment of defeat. . . . Hesitation was caused by Hall's movement and by the stubbornness of the 69th and 71st Penna."[203]

* * *

Immediately after Gettysburg, Webb was given command of the Second Division of the Second Corps until General Gibbon returned to duty the next spring. Webb received a head wound at the Battle of Spotsylvania Court House in May 1864 as a bullet struck the corner of his right eye. He returned to the army in January 1865 as chief of staff of the Army of the Potomac. His promotion included brevet major general and was assistant inspector general of the Military Division of the Atlantic at the conclusion of the Civil War. He was appointed military governor of the first military district of Virginia.

The *New York Times'* archives contain a published article that erroneously reported General Webb's death at Spotsylvania Court House in May 1864. The story's publication date was May 9, 1864. The headline was "Death of Gen. A. S. Webb."

The report of Thursday's battle includes news that Gen. ALEXANDER S. WEBB, commanding a brigade of the Second Division of the Second Army Corps, was among the killed. This is a serious loss to the army and the country. The service had few more capable officers, and none more promising. Gen. WEBB graduated at

West Point, we believe, in 1857, nearly at the head of his class. He was soon afterward ordered to Florida, and, after serving in that State for several months, was transferred to West Point, and with great credit filled the chair of an instructor. At the outbreak of the rebellion, he entered into active service at once, and fought as an artillery officer at the first battle of Manassas. Soon afterward, he had command of a volunteer infantry regiment, and in June, 1862, became attached to the staff of Gen. FITZJOHN PORTER, in the capacity of Inspector of the Fifth Army Corps. with the rank of Lieutenant-Colonel. In April, 1863, he was appointed Brigadier-General, on the recommendation of Gen. HOOKER, and was assigned to the command of a brigade in the Second Army Corps. At the battle of Gettysburg he displayed preeminent gallantry. Not a sing (sic) of Brigadier contributed so much, it is safe to say, to that great victory as young WEBB. He was in the very thickest of the fight, handled his men with extraordinary ability and coolness, and escaped death by a miracle, only to meet it among the first in the bloody work of the present year.

Gen. WEBB was not more than twenty-six years of age. He was a member of the Episcopal Church, and was a noble specimen of a Christian gentleman. In the highest degree generous, genial, courteous, truthful, brave, modest, of stainless honor, ever true to duty, he displayed the finest type of manhood. No nobler youth, no truer soldier, has fallen in this war.

Gen. WEBB was the youngest son of Gen. JAMES

WATSON WEBB, now Minister to Brazil. Soon after graduating, he married Miss ANNA REMSEN, of this City, and leaves, we believe, two or three children. The bereaved family will have the keenest public sympathy.[204]

Webb's active service concluded on December 5, 1870, and during his final year he was an instructor at West Point. After the service, Webb turned to education and became the second president of the City College of New York. He served from 1869 until 1902.

On October 16, 1898, the *New York Times* ran a long article on General Webb. The story began, "In a quaint and cozy office in the northwest corner of the old college building at Twenty-third Street and Lexington Avenue is found each day during school hours Gen. Alexander Steward Webb, the President of the College of the City of New York. Here for nearly thirty-three years—punctual, vigilant and exacting—he has directed the affairs of the institution that is dear to the hearts of many of the best-equipped and most useful citizens of this great metropolis. Not a few now prominent men can recall in mind days when they stood nervously before that long old-fashioned desk-table to 'report to the President' for some delinquency."[205]

The article describes Webb's work ethic at the college as the educational institution outgrew its buildings. The story notes that the college had 427 students and 27 instructors when Webb began his tenure and had grown to 1,700 students and 68 instructors. He is given credit for increasing the natural history collection of the school. The college also was known for educating the city's teachers.

The story says Webb "won distinction as a soldier, an instructor and as a writer."[206] As for Gettysburg, the story points out Webb's "gallant" conduct helped "stimulate" his troops to defend the Angle. The article also points out that Webb was a private man who didn't seek publicity.

Webb was awarded his Medal of Honor on September 28, 1891, for his service at Gettysburg. The citation read for "distinguished personal gallantry in leading his men forward at a critical period in the contest." The medal was awarded 28 years after the event and his retirement from service.

Webb also received his own statue at Gettysburg in 1915. The monument is placed near where he directed the Philadelphia Brigade during Pickett's Charge. Another statue of Webb was constructed on the campus of the City College of New York.

During the dedication of the first 72nd Pennsylvania monument at Gettysburg, which was more of a monument to the brigade rather than the regiment, on August 27, 1883, Webb was a featured speaker. He began his talk by saying, "These Cities of the Dead, established by the Government of the United States—preserved by the loving hands of those who cherish the saddest recollections of our late war—are the lasting monuments we have reared to testify to our assurance that it was God himself who preserved this Union; they are the pledges we have given that we will be its conservators.

198 · PICKETT'S CHARGE: THE UNTOLD STORY

"We, therefore, approach in reverential respect and affectionate regret the graves of our comrades who have fallen, and, with tender recollection of our last companionship with them, we drop the tear of pride—yes, but of glorious pride—when we recall the time and the circumstances of their death—the time of our own salvation."[207]

Why should those monuments be constructed? Webb asked and answered the question. He said, "If from these few words of mine we may find left with us the conviction that these cold marbles are not yet sufficient to record, with anything like fidelity, the magnitude of the services rendered by the men who fought on this spot, we will have done no more than simple justice to their patriotism in this our act of veneration."[208]

Webb recounted the 72nd Pennsylvania history, included Colonel Baxter recruiting the unit and the Civil War battles fought, including the Peninsula campaign, Antietam, Fair Oaks, Malvern Hill, Chancellorsville, and Fredericksburg.

The international impact of the Union victories at Gettysburg and Vicksburg was also addressed by Webb. The triumphs "made it necessary for these powers to continue dissimulation indefinitely." Webb went on to recount the actions of the Philadelphia Brigade during Gettysburg and called the battle, "in the political sense was, and is now throughout the world known to be the Waterloo of the Rebellion."[209]

During the talk, he gave credit to General Alexander Hays, "a glorious fighter," Colonel Norman Hall and others for their support of the Philadelphia Brigade.

Webb concluded his talk by speaking against the rebellion. "Brothers before the war—brothers today—we deplore the cause of these sad remembrances; but we well know as few others can, that mementos such as these must be erected that men may, in the sight of these hallowed graves, recall the errors of the past, and knowing the cost of rebellion against His will—resolve to foster and maintain the principles for which our fathers fought, for which their sons have died."[210]

Another civic activity by Webb included being treasurer of the Sanitary Aid Society of New York.

Webb died on February 12, 1911, in Riverdale, New York. He was just a few days away from his 76th birthday. He is buried in West Point National Cemetery. His wife, Anna Elizabeth Remsen Webb, died on November 15, 1912.

An article on Webb's death reported, "Webb and his wife, Anna Elizabeth nee Remsen, had eight children together. They married on November 28, 1855. After retiring from the U.S. Army, Webb returned to New York City and became president of the City College of New York, a position he would hold for 32 years. On September 28, 1891, General Webb received the highest military honor the United States awards—the Medal of Honor—for his brave leadership at the Battle of Gettysburg. The official citation reads, "Distinguished personal gallantry in leading his men forward at a critical period in the contest." Webb died on February 12, 1911 at Bronx, New York. He was 75 years old. He is a true American hero.

On February 16, 1911, the *New York Times* reported,

"Funeral services for Gen. Alexander S. Webb, who died at Riverdale, New York, on Sunday, were held yesterday at the Church of the Incarnation, Madison Avenue and thirty-sixth Street, New York. The coffin was covered with an American flag, on which rested a great cross of orchids, and many floral pieces had been sent to the church by relatives and friends. The memorial in the church to Admiral Farragut was decorated with flowers in recognition of the friendship of the two men.

"The honorary pallbearers were Gen. Frederick Dent Grant, Gen. Rodenbough, Gen. Pennington., Col. Larned, Major Lydecker, Col Wier, Darin P. Kingsley and Cleveland H. Dodge. The Legion of Honor, the Military Service Institution, and the College of the City of New York, of which Gen. Webb was ex-President, were represented by delegation." Among those who attended the services, according to the article, was General Daniel Sickles, who lost his leg at Gettysburg.

"The services were conducted by Rev. William M. Grosvenor, rector of the church. Webb was a communicant.

"At 1:30 p.m. a special train left the Grand Central Station with members of the family and the body of Gen. Webb for West Point. . . . (At West Point) the body was placed on a gun carriage and ferried to West Point. Drawn up in line, the corps of cadets stood at attention as the body passed, followed by a black-robed riderless horse, and the hills echoed with the salute of thirteen guns from the battery on the plains. . . . At the conclusion of a short burial service 'taps' broke the silence, and three volleys fired by the cadets once more resounded among the crags of old 'Cro' Nest' Mountain towering above the soldier's grave."[211]

* * *

Accolades for the Philadelphia Brigade and those Union officers, including Meade, Hancock and Gibbon, and men who fought at Gettysburg continued over the years. When the monument to the 69th Pennsylvania was dedicated in July 1887, Captain John E. Reilly said, "It was here you met the flower of the Confederate Army in hand to hand encounter, and here, many of our brave companions laid down their lives in that terrible struggle . . . when suddenly, about one o'clock belch forth its volcanic fire on your unprotected position . . . every missile known to modern warfare, were thrown against this position for two long hours; this was but the prelude to the most desperate infantry charge of modern times, for soon Pickett's Division was seen marching out from the shelter of yonder woods, with colors flying defiantly to the breeze, and seeming to say, 'We come to pierce your centre; match us if you can.'"[212]

Medal of Honor winner Colonel Wheelock Veazey of the 16th Connecticut recovered from his wounds and returned to Rutland, Connecticut, to continue his pursuit of practicing law. He became a state Supreme Court judge in 1879. He remained connected to the military through the GAR (Grand Army of the Republic) organization. He died on March 23, 1898, in Washington, D.C.

General Winfield Scott Hancock survived his wound at Gettysburg and returned to command for the Wilderness campaign but the injury caused him to vacate field command and to take command of the Veteran Reserve Corps at the end of the war. Hancock then assumed command of the Department of the East with headquarters at Governor's Island, New York. On April 21, 1866, Hancock received the thanks of Congress for his "skill and heroic valor" at Gettysburg.

During the election of 1880, Hancock ran unsuccessfully for President of the United States. He continued his military service until his death on February 9, 1886. He is buried in a family crypt at Norristown, Pennsylvania. General Abner Doubleday spoke at Hancock's service and said, "I can almost fancy I see Hancock again as he rode past the front of his commend, just previous to (Pickett's) assault, followed by a single orderly displaying his corps flag, while the missiles from a hundred pieces of artillery tore up the ground around him."

After the close of the Civil War, General Gibbon returned to regular army service and was assigned to command infantry units on the western plains, where he participated in numerous campaigns against plains tribes during several uprisings in the 1870's and 1880's. General Gibbon died in Baltimore, Maryland in 1891 and is interred in Arlington National Cemetery.

As for General Meade, he remained in command of the Army of the Potomac until the end of the Civil War but fought under the direction of General Ulysses S. Grant. His less than vigorous pursuit of the retreating troops of General Robert E. Lee's from Gettysburg doomed his chances for being placed in overall command of Northern forces. The War Department never considered him for such a post. At the conclusion of the war, Meade commanded the military division of the Atlantic while being headquartered in Philadelphia. Meade also served as a commissioner of Philadelphia's Fairmount Park. Two years after the war he commanded a district that included Alabama, Georgia and Florida. He died in 1872, at the age of 57, from pneumonia, reportedly connected to his Civil War wound received at White Oak Swamp. He is buried in Laurel Hill Cemetery, Philadelphia.

With the deaths of the enlisted men, stories of heroics at Gettysburg were detailed in obituaries. One such article was titled "Brave Veteran Dead—Charles O. Strayline Had Narrow Escape at Battle of Gettysburg." The obituary for the 68-year-old veteran stated, "Mr. Strayline was a veteran of the Civil War, having served in the 71st Pennsylvania Volunteers, formerly known as Colonel Baker's California Regiment. His brother George was made sergeant of the same regiment for bravery in the field. His brother Theodore was a member of Baxter's Zouaves, and was killed at Gettysburg. His father, at age 54, enlisted in 1862 in the 8th Pennsylvania Cavalry, and was discharged, after fighting for a year and a half, for disability.

"Charles Strayline and a party of the 71st had a narrow escape at Gettysburg. They managed to force their way over the stone wall at 'bloody angle' and were immediately captured by Pickett's brigade. The Confederates advised the prisoners to go to the rear and remain in safety. One half of the little band of heroes went, the others, among them Strayline, remained, and in about twenty minutes, when the wall was once more forced, they were recaptured together with a number of Pickett's men, by their friends."

* * *

Despite the many post-bellum accomplishments of the members of the Army of the Potomac, Gettysburg stands as their utmost contribution to the cause of the United States. The country would be far different without the sacrifices made by Meade, Hancock, Gibbon, Webb, members of the Philadelphia Brigade and all of the other soldiers defending the Angle against Pickett's Charge.

Victory, not only at Gettysburg but the whole Civil War, was within the grasp of Robert E. Lee at Gettysburg. The bravery of the Union line officers and their men defeated a determined Confederate force While the Union's winning the Civil War was almost two years distant, defeat was at hand on the hot afternoon of July 3, 1863, at Gettysburg.

Webb and all of the defenders of Pickett's Charge were true American heroes.

SECOND ARMY CORPS ORGANIZATION

Maj. General Winfield S. Hancock;
Brig. General John Gibbon

First Division	Brig. General John C. Caldwell
First Brigade	Col. Edward E. Cross Colonel H. Boyd McKeen
5th New Hampshire	Lt. Col. Charles E. Hapgood
61st New York	Col. K. Oscar Broady
81st Pennsylvania	Lt. Col. Amos Stroh
148th Pennsylvania	Col. H. Boyd McKeen Lieut. Col. Robert McFarlane
Second Brigade	Colonel Patrick Kelly
28th Massachusetts	Col. Richard Byrnes
63rd New York (2 cos.)	Lt. Col. Richard C. Bently Capt. Thomas Touhy
69th New York (2 cos.)	Capt. Richard Moroney Lt. James J. Smith
88th New York (2 cos.)	Capt. Denis F. Burke
116th Pennsylvania (4 cos.)	Maj. St. Clair A. Mulholland
Third Brigade	Colonel Samuel K. Zook Lt. Colonel John Fraser
52nd New York	Lt. Col. Charles G. Freudenberg Capt. William Scherrer

(continued)

First Division , Third Brigade (continued)

57th New York	Lt. Col. Alford B. Chapman
66th New York	Col. Orlando H. Morris Lt. Col. John S. Hammell Maj. Peter Nelson
140th Pennsylvania	Col. Richard P. Roberts Lt. Col. John Fraser

Fourth Brigade	Colonel John R. Brooke
27th Connecticut (2 cos.)	Lt. Col. Henry C. Merwin Maj. James H. Coburn
2nd Delaware	Col. William P. Baily Capt. Charles H. Christman
64th New York	Col. Daniel G. Bingham Maj. Leman W. Bradley
53rd Pennsylvania	Lt. Col. Richard McMichael
145th Pennsylvania (7 cos.)	Col. Hiram L. Brown Capt. John W. Reynolds Capt. Moses W. Oliver

Second Division	Brig. General John Gibbon Brig. General William Harrow.

First Brigade	Brig. General William Harrow Colonel Francis E. Heath
19th Maine	Col. Francis E. Heath Lt. Col. Henry W. Cunningham
15th Massachusetts	Col. George H. Ward Lt. Col. George C. Joslin
1st Minnesota (inc. 2nd Co. Minnesota Sharpshooters)	Col. William Colvill, Jr. Capt. Nathan S. Messick Capt. Henry C. Coates

(continued)

Second Division , First Brigade *(continued)*

82nd New York (2nd Militia)	Lt. Col. James Huston Capt. John Darrow

Second Brigade	Brig. General Alexander S. Webb
69th Pennsylvania	Col. Dennis O'Kane Capt. William Davis
71st Pennsylvania	Col. Richard Penn Smith
72nd Pennsylvania	Col. De Witt C. Baxter Lt. Col. Theodore Hesser
106th Pennsylvania	Lieut. Col. William L. Curry

Third Brigade	Colonel Norman J. Hall
19th Massachusetts	Col. Arthur F. Devereux
20th Massachusetts	Col. Paul J. Revere Lt. Col. George N. Macy Capt. Henry L. Abbott
7th Michigan	Lt. Col. Amos E. Steele, Jr. Maj. Sylvanus W. Curtis
42nd New York	Col. James E. Mallon
59th New York(4 cos.)	Lieut. Col. Max A. Thoman Capt. William McFadden
1st Co., Massachusetts Sharpshooters (Unattached)	Capt. William Plumer Lt. Emerson L. Bicknell

Third Division	Brig. General Alexander Hays
First Brigade	Colonel Samuel S. Carroll
14th Indiana	Col. John Coons
4th Ohio	Lt. Col. Leonard W. Carpenter

(continued)

Third Division , First Brigade *(continued)*

8th Ohio	Lt. Col. Franklin Sawyer
7th West Virginia	Lt. Col. Jonathan H. Lockwood
Second Brigade	Colonel Thomas A. Smyth Lt. Colonel Francis E. Pierce
14th Connecticut	Maj. Theodore G. Ellis
1st Delaware	Lt. Col. Edward P. Harris Capt. Thomas B. Hizar Lt. William Smith Lt. John D. Dent
12th New Jersey	Maj. John T. Hill
10th New York Bn	Maj. George F. Hopper
108th New York	Lt. Col. Francis E. Pierce
Third Brigade	Colonel George L. Willard Colonel Eliakim Sherrill Lt. Col. James L. Bull
39th New York(4 cos.)	Maj. Hugo Hildebrandt
111th New York	Col. Clinton D. MacDougall Lt. Col. Isaac M. Lusk Capt. Aaron B. Seeley
125th New York	Lt. Col. Levin Crandell
126th New York	Col. Eliakim Sherrill Lt. Col. James L. Bull
Artillery Brigade	Capt. John G. Hazard
Battery G, 1st New York Light and 14th New York Battery	Lt. Albert S. Sheldon Capt. James M. Rorty Lt. Robert E. Rogers
Battery A, 1st Rhode Island	Capt. William A. Arnold

(continued)

Third Division , Artillery Brigade *(continued)*

Battery B, 1st Rhode Island	Lt. T. Fred Brown
Battery I, 1st United States	Lt. George A. Woodruff
	Lt. Tully McCrea
Battery A, 4th United States	Lt. Alonzo H. Cushing
	Sgt. Frederick Fuger

NOTES

Chapter 1

1. Supreme Court of Pennsylvania, *Trial of the Survivors of the 72nd Pennsylvania Versus The Gettysburg Battlefield Memorial Association*, (Harrisburg, PA: 1891), xcv.
2. Ibid.
3. *New York City College Quarterly*, (New York, N.Y.), Volume 7, Page 4.
4. Larry Tagg, *The Generals of Gettysburg*, (Garden City, NY: Da Capo Press, 1998), 49.

Chapter 2

5. Don Ernsberger, *At The Wall: The 69th Pennsylvania Irish Volunteers At Gettysburg* (Xlibris, 2006), 38.
6. Walter Fox, *Dennis O'Kane and the 69th Pennsylvania Volunteers: Facing Lee's Best Troops They Stood Their Ground* (Irish edition, Philadelphia, June 1999).
7. Gary G. Lash, *The History of Edward Baker's California Regiment (71st Pa)* (Butternut and Blue Press, 2001), 325-326.
8. Stephen B. Oates, *With Malice Towards None: The Life of Abraham Lincoln* (Harper & Row, New York, 1977), 64.
9. Ibid., 263.
10. Ibid.
11. E. B. Long, *The Civil War Day By Day* (Doubleday, Garden City, NY, 1971), 367.
12. National Park Service, Gettysburg, (NPS), Wistar files.
13. Ibid., Bachelder Papers.
14. Ibid.
15. War of the Rebellion Official Records (OR) (Washington, D.C.), Series 1, Volume 27, 60

16. Ibid.
17. Freeman Cleaves, *Meade of Gettysburg* (University of Oklahoma Press, Norman, OK), 118.
18. Ibid.
19. Mark M. Boatner III, *The Civil War Dictionary* (David McKay Company, Inc. New York, NY, 1959), 539.
20. Lash, *The History of Edward Baker's California Regiment (71ˢᵗ Pa)*, 327.
21. Joseph R. C. Ward, *History of the 106ᵗʰ Pennsylvania* (Grant, Faires & Rodgers, Philadelphia, PA, 1883), 150.
22. Lash, *The History of Edward Baker's California Regiment (71ˢᵗ Pa)*, 329.
23. Ibid.
24. Ward, *History of the 106ᵗʰ Pennsylvania*, 149
25. Anthony W. McDermott, Sixty-Ninth Regiment, Pennsylvania Veteran Volunteers, To the Ancient Order of Hibernians, (D. J. Gallagher Company, Philadelphia, PA, 1889).
26. OR, Series I, Volume 27, 367.
27. Ward, *History of the 106ᵗʰ Pennsylvania*, 157.
28. Frank Haskell, *The Battle of Gettysburg* (Commandery of the State of Massachusetts, Military Order of the Loyal Legion of the United States, 1908), 15.
29. McDermott, Sixty-Ninth Regiment, Pennsylvania Veteran Volunteers, To the Ancient Order of Hibernians.

Chapter 3
30. NPS, Bachelder papers.
31. Ibid.
32. Lash, *The History of Edward Baker's California Regiment (71ˢᵗ Pa)*, 334.
33. OR, Series 1, Volume 27, 427.
34. Ibid., 334, 335.
35. OR, Series 1, Volume 27, 372.

36. Ibid., 416.
37. Ibid.
38. NPS.

Chapter 4

39. Haskell, *The Battle of Gettysburg*, 15.
40. NPS.
41. Bortner, *The Civil War Dictionary*, 41.
42. Haskell, *The Battle of Gettysburg*, 36.
43. Ibid., 34-37.
44. OR, Series I, Volume 27, 73-74.
45. Haskell, *The Battle of Gettysburg*, 38
46, Ibid., 43.
47. Ibid., 46.
48. OR, Series I, Volume 27, 372.
49. NPS.
50. Ibid.

Chapter 5

51. Lash, *The History of Edward Baker's California Regiment (71st Pa)*, 337.
52. Ibid.
53. Ibid.
54. Stephen W. Sears, *Gettysburg* (New York, Houghton Mifflin Company, 2003), 396.
55. Carol Reardon, *Pickett's Charge in History and Memory*, (Chapel Hill, N.C., The University of North Carolina Press, 1977), 10.
56. James G. Biddle, *Gettysburg Annals of the War* (Philadelphia, The Times Publishing Co. 1879), 213.
57. NPS.
58. Haskell, *The Battle of Gettysburg*, 48.
59. Ibid., 52,

60. NPS.
61. Haskell, *The Battle of Gettysburg*, 52.
62. NPS, Bachelder Papers.
63. NPS.
64. D. Scott Hartwig, *It Struck Horror to Us All*, Gettysburg Magazine, Issue 4, January 1991.
65. Ibid.
66. Haskell, *The Battle of Gettysburg*, 53.
67. Winfield Scott Hancock Historical Society.
68. NPS.
69. Ibid.
70. Sears, *Gettysburg*, 400.
71. Ibid.
72. NPS, Bachelder Papers.
73. Ibid.
74. Ibid.
75. Ibid.
76. OR, Series I, Volume 27, 372, 373.
77. Sears, *Gettysburg*, 409.
78. Lash, *The History of Edward Baker's California Regiment (71st Pa)*, 338.
79. Ernsberger, *At The Wall*, 91.
80. OR, Series 1, Volume 27, Part 1, 428.
81. Ibid, 437.
82. Haskell, *The Battle of Gettysburg*, 56.

Chapter 6

83. Sears, *Gettysburg*, 409.
84. Haskell, *The Battle of Gettysburg*, 56.
85. NPS.
86. Fox, *Dennis O'Kane and the 69th Pennsylvania Volunteers*.
87. Ibid.
88. Hartwig, *It Struck Horror To Us All*

89. Ibid.
90. NPS.
91. NPS, Federick Fuger files.
92. Sears, *Gettysburg*, 411.
93. Ibid.
94. Ibid.
95. Hartwig, *It Struck Horror To Us All*
96. OR, Series 1, Volume 27, Part 1, 437.
97. NPS, John Gibbon, *Personal Reflections on the Civil War.*
98. Haskell, *The Battle of Gettysburg*, 56.
99. OR, Series 1, Volume 27, Part 1, 437.
100. Lash, *The History of Edward Baker's California Regiment (71ˢᵗ Pa)*, 338.
101. Ibid.
102. OR, Series 1, Volume 27, Part 1, 373.

Chapter 7

103. NPS.
104. Ibid.
105. Pennsylvania Supreme Court, 135.
106. Lash, *The History of Edward Baker's California Regiment (71ˢᵗ Pa)*, 340
107. NPS, Bachelder Papers.
108. Ibid
109. Lash, *The History of Edward Baker's California Regiment (71ˢᵗ Pa)*, 343.
110. NPS, Bachelder Papers.
111. OR, Series 1, Volume 27, Part 1, 349, 350.
112. NPS, John Gibbon, *Personal Reflections on the Civil War.*
113. OR, Series 1, Volume 27, Part 1, 374.
114. NPS.
115. Ibid., Bachelder Papers.
116. Ibid.

117. Ibid.
118. NPS.
119. NPS, Bachelder Papers.
120. Ward, Joseph R. C., History of the 106th Pennsylvania, P166.
121. NPS Bachelder *The Bachelder Papers: Gettysburg in Their Own Words*, 378.
122. Haskell, *The Battle of Gettysburg*, 56.
123. Ibid., 57.
124. Ibid.
125. NPS
126. NPS, Bachelder Papers.
127. Hartwig, *It Struck Horror to Us All*.
128. Fox, *Dennis O'Kane and the 69th Pennsylvania Volunteers: Facing Lee's Best Troops They Stood Their Ground*.
128. Ibid.
129. NPS
130. OR, Series 1, Volume 27, Part 1, 374.
131. NPS, Bachelder Papers.
132. Hartwig, *It Struck Horror to Us All*.
133. NPS, Bachelder Papers.
134. Sears, *Gettysburg*, 452.
135. Ibid.
136. Ibid.
137. *Baltimore American and Commercial Advertiser, August 6, 1863, edition.*
138. OR, Series 1, Volume 27, Part 1, 373.
139. Jordan, David, *Winfield Scott Hancock: A Soldier's Life*, (Indiana University Press, 1995).

Chapter 8

140. Sears, *Gettysburg*, 469.
141. NPS, Bachelder Papers.
142. NPS.

143. Ibid.
144. Ibid.
145. Ibid.
146. Ibid.
147. Sears, *Gettysburg*, 435.
148. NPS
149. OR, Series 1, Volume 27, Part 1, 350.
150. Ibid., 418
151. Ibid., 376
152. Ward, *History of the 106th PA Volunteers*, 262.
153. OR, Series 1, Volume 27, Part 1, 375.
154. Sears, *Gettysburg*, 469
155. NPS
156. Ibid.
157. Ibid.
158. Freedoms Foundation.
159. OR, Series 1, Volume 27, Part 1, 374.
160. NPS.
161. Ibid.
162. Ibid, Bachelder Papers.
163. NPS.

Chapter 9

164. Pennsylvania, Supreme Court, viii.
165. Ibid.
166. Ibid., xciv.
167. NPS. Bachelder Papers.
168. Ibid.
169. Pennsylvania Supreme Court, vii.
170. Ibid., 34.
171. Ibid., 35
172. Ibid., xlii.
173. Ibid., xli.

174. Ibid., xli.
175. Ibid., 43.
176. Ibid., 49.
177. Ibid., 56.
178. Ibid., 63.
179. Ibid., 76.
180. Ibid., 81.
181. Ibid., xlii.
182. Ibid., xlii.
183. NPS, Bachelder Papers.
184. Pennsylvania Supreme Court, 136.
185. Ibid., 150.
186. Ibid., 137.
187. Ibid., 138.
188. Ibid., cvi.
189. Ibid., 85.
190. Ibid., 125.
191. Ibid., 116.
192. Ibid., 159.
193. Ibid., 161.
194. Ernsberger, *At the Wall*, 120.
195. *Gettysburg Compiler*, June 7, 1887.
196. Ibid.
197. Ibid.
198. Ibid.
199. Ibid.
200. NPS.
201. Ibid., Bachelder Papers.

Chapter 10

202. NPS.
203. Ibid.
204. *New York Times*, May 9, 1864.

205. Ibid, October 16, 1898.
206. Ibid.
207. NPS.
208. Ibid.
209. Ibid.
210. Ibid.
211. *New York Times*, February 16, 1911.
212. McDermott, *Sixty-Ninth Regiment, Pennsylvania Veteran Volunteers, To the Ancient Order of Hibernians.*

BIBLIOGRAPHY

Bachelder, Colonel John Bachelder, *The Bachelder Papers: Gettysburg in Their Own* Words. Dayton, Ohio; Morningside Press, 1994.

Bachelder Papers, National Park Service, Gettysburg.

Boatner, Mark M. III, *The Civil War Dictionary*. New York, N.Y., David McKay Company, Inc., 1959.

Busey, John, *Regimental Strengths & Losses at Gettysburg*, Hightstown, N.J., Longstreet House, 1982.

Cleaver, Freeman, *Meade of Gettysburg*. Norman, Oklahoma, University of Oklahoma Press, 1960.

Coddington, Edwin B., *The Gettysburg Campaign: A Study in Command*. New York, N.Y., Touchstone of Simon and Schuster, 1997.

Coffin, Charles C., *Eyewitness to Gettysburg*. Shippensburg, Pa., Burd Street Press, 1997.

Ernsberger, Don, *At The Wall: The 69th Pennsylvania "Irish Volunteers" At Gettysburg*, Xlibris Corp., 2006.

Fox, Walter, *Dennis O'Kane and the 69th Pennsylvania Volunteers: Facing Lee's Best Troops They Stood Their Ground*. Philadelphia, Pa., Irish edition, 1999.

Gallagher, Gary W., editor, *The Third Day at Gettysburg & Beyond*. Chapel Hill, N.C., The University of North Carolina Press, 1994.

Gibbon, General John, *Personal Recollections of the Civil War*. New York, N.Y., G. P. Putnam's Sons, 1928.

Gottfried, Bradley M., *Stopping Pickett: The History of the Philadelphia Brigade*. Shippensburg, Pa; White Mane Books, 1999.

Hartwig, D. Scott, *It Struck Horror To Us All*, Gettysburg, Pa., *Gettysburg Magazine*, Issue 4, January 1, 1991.

Haskell, Frank Aretas, *The Battle of Gettysburg*. Boston, Mass.,

Commandery of the State of Massachusetts, Military Order of the Loyal Legion of the United States, 1908.

Haskell, Frank A. and Coates, William, *Gettysburg*. New York, N.Y., Bantam Books, 1992.

Hess, Earl J., *Pickett's Charge: The Last Attack at Gettysburg*. Chapel Hill, N.C., The University of North Carolina Press, 2001.

Jamieson, Perry D., *Winfield Scott Hancock Gettysburg Hero*. Abilene, Texas, McWhiney Foundation Press, 2003.

Jones, John B., *A Rebel War Clerk's Diary*. New York, N.Y., A. S. Barnes & Company, 1961.

Jordan, David M. *Winfield Scott Hancock: A Soldier's Life*. Bloomington, Indiana, Indiana University Press, 1988.

Lash, Gary G., *The History of Edward Baker's California Regiment (71st Pa.)*. Baltimore, Md., Butternut and Blue Press, 2001.

Long, E. B., *The Civil War Day By Day, An Almanac 1861-1865*. Garden City, NY; Doubleday & Company, Inc., 1971.

Oates, Stephen B., *With Malice Towards None: The Life of Abraham Lincoln*, New York, N.Y.; Harper & Row, 1977.

Reardon, Carol, *Pickett's Charge In History & Memory*, Chapel Hill, N.C., The University of North Carolina Press, 1977.

Rollins, Richard, editor, *Pickett's Charge!: Eyewitness Accounts*. Redondo Beach, California, Rank and File Publications, 1994.

Sears, Stephen W. *Gettysburg*, New York, N.Y., Houghton Mifflin Company, 2003.

Stackpole, Edward J., *They Met At Gettysburg*. Harrisburg, Pa., Stackpole Books, 1982.

Stewart, George R., *Pickett's Charge: A microhistory of the final attack at Gettysburg, July 3, 1863*. Boston, Mass., Houghton Mifflin Company, 1959.

Tagg, Larry, *The Generals of Gettysburg, The Leaders of America's Greatest Battles*. Cambridge, MA; Da Capo Press, 1998.

Ward, Joseph R. C. *History of the 106th Pennsylvania*, Philadelphia, Grant, Faires & Rodgers, 1883.

War of Rebellion Official Records of the Union and Confederate Armies. Washington, D.C., Government Printing Office, 1889.

Written by Leading Participants, *Annals of War.* Philadelphia, Pennsylvania, The Times Publishing Company, 1879.

INDEX

and defeating Pickett's
Charge, 1–2
describes meeting at
Leister farm, 56–62
letter to wife, 67
lunch with George Meade,
63–64
observations of, 47
and report after artillery
barrage, 103
and report on artillary
barrage, 74
at "The Angle", 97
wounds of, 118–120
writings about the
Southerners, 109–110
Gordon, John B., 79
Grant, Ulysses S., 26, 148,
202
Greene, George Sears, 44
Grimes, James W., 160

H
Hall, Norman J., 62, 90, 98,
101, 130, 138
Halleck, Henry, 21, 24–26
Hancock, Winfield Scott
death of, 202
and formation of defense
line, 32
life after the war, 201
and meeting at Leister
farm, 55–62

nicknamed "Hancock the
Superb", 79
observations on Pickett's
Charge, 105–107
and report on fighting at
Culp's Hill, 46–47
and troops on Cemetery
Hill, 1–2
writings about Gibbon's
wounds, 120
Harpers Ferry, 15, 21, 24–25
Harrow, William, 41–42, 99,
120
Hart, Patrick, 82
Harvey, John Jr., 78
Haskell, Frank Aretas
on advancement of the
enemy, 93–94
and description of Union
shelling, 72
and his account of
Gettysburg, 130–131
and lunch with Meade and
Gibbon, 64
and Meade's headquarters,
34
and meeting at Leister
farm, 57–62
Hays, Alexander, 47, 65, 99,
140
Head, Edward, 101
"High Water Mark of the
Confederacy", 1, 36, 128